The Essential Guide to Assertiveness

How to Speak Up for Yourself,
Stop People-Pleasing, and Win Respect in
Your Life and Relationships

James Turnbull

LIBRITO

For permission requests and further information on Librito's other products, please contact info@libritopublishing.com.

ISBN: Paperback 978-1-8384222-2-6 | eBook 978-1-8384222-3-3

PAPERBACK EDITION
libritopublishing.com

This book is dedicated to everyone on their journey to assertiveness.

Contents

Introduction
An Overview of Assertiveness

Do you feel guilt, fear, or awkwardness when you try to stand your ground? Are you tired of letting things go because you are worried about asking for what you want? Do you want to stop remaining agreeable all the time because it is complicating your way of life?

If you answered 'yes' to the above questions, you are struggling with assertiveness. It is quite common to feel this way, and you certainly are not alone. Assertiveness is nothing more than a style of communication that empowers and teaches you to speak up for yourself, stand up for everything you believe in, and do it respectfully. It allows you to confidently express what you need or desire without feeling a compulsive need to explain yourself. Learning to be assertive means the adeptness to communicate what you want whilst being considerate of the opinions, thoughts, and beliefs of others.

Assertiveness is one of the most important social skills you can learn. You cannot be your true self unless you can freely communicate your wants, desires, thoughts, and feelings.

Assertiveness increases your self-esteem and gives you the confidence required to speak your mind without losing someone's respect. It enhances your decision-making skills, reduces stress and anguish, and helps you to understand what you truly need and want in life. Assertiveness gives you the confidence required to face conflicts and problems head-on and confidently stand by your decisions. It teaches you to accept responsibility for everything you say and do. When you start living your life assertively, attaining your goals and dreams becomes easier.

If assertiveness is that important, why do so many people struggle with it? Most causes are associated with core beliefs formed from childhood conditioning, life experiences, and our general personalities. This social anxiety inhibits effective communication with others and the ability to express our own feelings and beliefs. Perhaps it is a fear of upsetting others, disconnecting from loved ones, or struggling with low self-confidence and self-worth. Whatever the reason, it ultimately reduces the ability to express ourselves without restriction. If this becomes the norm, life cannot be enjoyed and lived to the fullest.

Are you wondering how I know all this? Well, I am speaking from personal experience. For as long as I can remember, I struggled with assertiveness. I thought it was a gift bestowed only on a lucky few. It felt like I never lived for myself, from trying to please everyone to severely depending on external validation. This was when I had a 'eureka' moment. Finally, I stumbled upon the realization that the only person I was responsible for was myself. I realized it was impossible to please everyone, and if I did try, I would only make myself miserable. I started focusing on myself, building my confidence, and learning to become assertive. The results were life-changing!

During my teenage years and into adulthood, I distinctly remember the difficulty I experienced sharing my thoughts, beliefs, and opinions. I avoided contributing to classroom discussions at school for fear of giving the wrong answer and humiliating myself. I yearned the teacher would overlook me when randomly selecting someone from the class to answer a question. I did not command respect from my peers and often was at the receiving end of cruel pranks. This lack of self-esteem and confidence continued at university when I was uncomfortable contributing to group discussions or communicating my feelings. I entered working life struggling to refute someone else's viewpoint because I was worried about creating conflicts or starting arguments. In fact, I was so concerned about upsetting others it resulted in me seldom speaking my mind. It was a long time before finally accepting I was struggling to express myself. But why am I telling you all of this? The reason is that retrospectively I can now look back at those times and fully understand how assertiveness could have set me on a different trajectory in life from an earlier age.

In this book, you will learn about the meaning of assertiveness, its advantages, the barriers, and practical tips to grow and develop this skill. Do not feel overwhelmed looking at all the topics you need to cover. Think of this process as a journey. It is my sincere wish the content within these pages will guide you every step of the way. At various points, you will find thought-provoking activities titled 'Your Journey'. Please do not skip over these tasks but take the time to work through them carefully. An important aspect of assertiveness is self-introspection and self-awareness, and these activities are designed to help you on your voyage of discovery. Becoming assertive is possible provided you commit to the process and are willing to learn, change, and grow.

Chapter 1
Understanding Assertiveness

Let us start by running through the four styles of communication and briefly explain the traits of each:

- Passive.
- Aggressive.
- Passive-aggressive.
- Assertive.

Passive communicators typically struggle to establish boundaries in relationships. They are anxious and insecure to the extent they cannot stand up for themselves or express what they truly desire. Such people stay far from confrontations, cannot express their opinions adequately, and are excessive apologists. However, they can subtly violate the rights and values of others, too, by not respecting their wishes or needs.

Those with aggressive communication styles usually express their feelings, beliefs, or thoughts in a way that seems threatening to others. Aggressive communication is used to establish control by demonstrating dominance and power. Those who favour this communication style usually make incessant requests and order others around. They are also adept at accusing and blaming people or the situation itself rather than accepting their mistakes.

Those with passive-aggressive communication styles are usually prone to making sarcastic and ironic remarks. They seldom express their opinions publicly. They do not show their true feelings and accuse others whenever they are frustrated.

On the other hand, assertiveness is the ability to respect yourself, communicate directly, accept responsibility for your mistakes, and express your feelings. Assertive people can control themselves in every situation and resolve conflicts calmly. They are skilled at articulating their disagreement and have healthy levels of self-confidence.

When you look at an assertive individual, it can be quite easy to believe they were born with it. However, the good news is assertiveness is a skill that can be learned and developed. But what are the elements of assertive behaviour?

To begin with, assertive people understand respect is a two-way street. The simple truth is if you want respect, it must be earned by conducting yourself in a mutually considerate manner.

Self-acceptance is key to becoming assertive. It means you have observed, evaluated, and learned how to cultivate and maintain a positive inner dialogue, accepted yourself for who you are, acknowledged your flaws, and understand that perfection is a mirage: something that can never be materialized. This knowledge about yourself increases your understanding and awareness, leading to greater self-respect. In turn, it guides you towards humility because you understand we are all human and inherently flawed.

A primary characteristic of assertiveness is the ability to prioritize and foster positive relationships with almost anyone easily. It is a simple fact that effective relationships cannot be based on lies, dishonesty, or hypocrisy in any form. Assertiveness is staying true to your identity and upholding your beliefs without sacrificing individualism or fearing discord.

Most problems are usually the result of miscommunication or some form of communication gap. It is only effective and efficient communication that can resolve them. This requires self-awareness and self-reflection. These traits make it easier to express yourself clearly, truthfully, and unambiguously. Effective communication is not only about talking and sharing; it is also about active listening. Assertiveness is an awareness of the true value of communication.

Regulating emotions and staying in control of your attitude is fundamental to developing assertiveness. It is an awareness that we all have emotions and feelings that need to be processed. We all experience uncomfortable emotions such as pain, anger, anxiety, or frustration, but assertiveness simply means learning to control these feelings rather than becoming overwhelmed by them. It is the ability to empathize with others instead of fanning the flame or exploring any weaknesses that can be manipulated. When you are assertive, you do not blame anyone else; emotional stability allows you the power to empathize with others whilst standing your ground.

The reality of life is you cannot cultivate perfect relationships with everyone around you. At times, you will encounter others who are inclined to take you for granted, abuse the relationship you share with them, or even desire to harm you. All this tends to create unnecessary stress and tension in your life. When you are assertive, you are aware of your limits and are not scared of establishing boundaries. This essentially means you are not afraid of saying, "That's enough." Every situation has a limit, and you have the right to establish personal boundaries. There must be an understanding and acceptance that we are incapable of living up to the expectations or desires of others in every single situation. Assertiveness is the ability to say 'no' without any unnecessary conflict.

Emotional independence is the quality of regulating your emotions even during difficult situations. It means you can control your emotions without relying on or seeking constant approval, validation, and attention from others. Assertiveness is the ability to tolerate and deal with rejection or indifference from others without taking it personally. It is the ability to live your life based on your own convictions, beliefs, and needs. It does not mean you do not want to be acknowledged by others. It simply suggests you are emotionally strong enough to understand external approval does not define you.

Your Journey

It is time for a little self-introspection. This exercise does not serve any purpose if you cannot be open with yourself. Review the components of assertive behaviour above. There should be seven qualities in total:

- Respect for others.
- Self-acceptance.
- Foster positive relationships.
- Effective communication.
- Ability to regulate emotions and control attitude.
- Establishing boundaries.
- Emotional independence.

Ask yourself if you possess the different qualities listed above. Draw a table with two columns and write down those attributes you possess on the left-hand side and those you will need to develop on the right. Think of examples you can use to support your decision for placing each of the seven qualities in each category.

If you are struggling to find the answers, you can ask your loved ones for their insights. This simple exercise will increase your self-awareness. After all, unless you are aware of the problem, you cannot solve it!

Chapter 2
The Benefits of Assertiveness

There are many benefits to assertiveness that you will connect with and apply to your everyday life, from self-awareness and emotional clarity to stress reduction and productivity.

Assertiveness allows you to concentrate on yourself and how your thoughts, actions, and emotions affect your life. When you are self-aware, it becomes easier to manage your feelings, ensures your efforts are in sync with your values and gives you a chance to evaluate your life. It teaches you to be proactive, increases self-acceptance, and promotes growth and development. It allows you to view circumstances from other people's perspectives, not believing your opinion is the only one available. Self-awareness is the first step to understanding who you are as a person.

As part of the human fraternity, we are inherently social creatures. Relationships are present in all aspects of our lives; they cannot be avoided, nor should we consciously side-step them. Learning to develop healthy relationships is important for your mental and emotional well-being. When positive people surround you, mean you well, and love you, you will instinctively feel better about yourself.

Rather than believing true happiness lies in making others happy or chasing validation, emotional clarity teaches you to look within. By paying attention to your true self and acknowledging your wants and needs, it becomes easier to understand your emotions. Instead of invalidating or ignoring them, assertiveness teaches you to recognise, understand, and accept them. When you have this clarity, your emotional health improves, making it easier to regulate your emotions.

By learning to stand up and voice your views, you will feel better about yourself. This simple act will increase your self-confidence. If you start trusting your ability to get things done, your confidence levels will rise. When you are confident about yourself, it shows in all aspects of your life, increasing your self-worth and reducing negative thoughts.

Assertiveness offers better insight into what is and is not acceptable to you. It helps establish and maintain healthy boundaries. These boundaries are your limits. Anything that violates these limits or pushes you past your breaking point is in direct violation of your core beliefs and values.

The inability to say 'no' can be the source of incredible stress by needlessly increasing your responsibilities and burdens. We lead hectic lives, and there is no reason for additional pressures. The inability to say 'no' pushes you past your breaking point and violates your boundaries. If you have any people-pleasing or approval-seeking tendencies, saying 'no' can seem impossible. Assertiveness gives you the necessary self-awareness to understand your limitations and capabilities and the direction to say 'yes' or 'no.'

One of the most common reasons for increased stress, especially in relationships, is miscommunication. Suppose you stop expressing yourself because, inwardly, there is a worry about displeasing people, or perhaps you only voice opinions that others will accept. In that case, the only person you are deceiving is yourself. This is the primary reason for increasing resentment, frustration, and annoyance. A relationship should never be a source of all these undesirable emotions. When you can express yourself distinctly and without any ambiguity, your expectations become clear. It not only shows what you want, but it tells others how they should or should not behave towards you.

Certain conversations are inherently unpleasant. Such exchanges include giving negative feedback, conflict resolution, and addressing topics that can result in a confrontation. You cannot ignore these conversations or put them on hold until later. If you avoid them, they can become much more problematic. Assertiveness equips you with the skills required to navigate such talks without escalation or hurting anyone involved, including yourself. In a way, it helps create win-win situations.

Expressing yourself and standing up for what you believe in means you cannot ignore others. Rather, you can respectfully ask for everything you need. This increases the chances of others listening to you. The health of your relationships improves when they are based on respect and understanding.

Your decision-making skills are enhanced when you are aware of your wants, needs, and desires. This, coupled with increased self-awareness, especially in your beliefs and values, makes it easier to consider if your decisions are in sync with your principles; therefore, using this insight increases the chance of making better choices.

Chapter 3
Barriers to Assertiveness

A common reason many people shy away from assertiveness is the fear of disconnecting from their social network. There is a concern others will not like them if they express their wants, needs and desires. If you do not express yourself for fear of conflict or distance in relationships, then you cannot be true to yourself.

A problem most of us face is difficulty articulating our thoughts and feelings. A common barrier to assertiveness is vagueness or passiveness concerning what we need or want. The good news is you can easily overcome this with a little practice. Unless you are emotionally aware, you cannot express your feelings efficiently. Are you worried about letting others know what you want because you do not think they will understand? Or perhaps you were labelled as overly sensitive or too touchy growing up, and this prevents you from expressing your emotions? Adults are usually quite conscious about how they convey their feelings. This is due to societal conditioning. Unfortunately, most of us were taught certain emotions are 'good' while others are 'bad.' If you feel emotionally overwhelmed, the ability to express your feelings efficiently will be decreased. To develop emotional awareness, start acknowledging your feelings and emotions without any judgement. Understand there is no such thing as good or bad feelings. All that matters is how you respond to them. Avoid ignoring and suppressing your emotions. Accept them, question where they originate and carefully answer them. You will learn more about how to do this in the subsequent chapters.

How can you be assertive when you struggle with a low opinion of yourself and believe you do not deserve anything good in life? The problem lies with negative core beliefs deeply rooted in our psyche based on childhood experiences or relationship patterns. Such negative thoughts manifest as a lack of self-worth. You can improve your positive self-image by learning to assert your opinions, quit people-pleasing, and protect your boundaries.

Assertiveness is all about expressing your thoughts, feelings, beliefs, and needs. However, at times you may not be aware of what you truly want. Different reasons can prevent you from understanding what you desire. Perhaps you are too busy concentrating on others or living your life on autopilot due to the many and varied commitments in your diary. Whatever the reason, you cannot confidently express yourself without first clearly understanding in your own mind your wants and needs.

Similarly, you cannot assuredly ask for what you want if you believe your needs do not matter. This sort of thinking will prevent you from ever expressing your desires. Whether it is societal conditioning or childhood experiences, different factors may condition you into believing your needs are secondary. If you start living your life in this way, you can never be fully expressive. Unless you acknowledge your needs and realize they are important, it is impossible to become assertive.

Apart from low self-worth, a lack of confidence in yourself and your abilities can prevent you from developing assertiveness. If you cannot be decisive or clearly express your needs, it is difficult for others to feel sure about you or the words you are communicating. Most of us usually harbour such insecurities stemming from negative beliefs or ideas of unhealthy perfection. You can also feel insecure about your abilities when you fail, experience setbacks, and encounter obstacles in life. The suggestions and practices in Chapters 4-12 are designed to improve self-confidence and self-esteem.

It can become quite challenging to think rationally when you feel anxious. When you feel triggered, your fight or flight response takes over. If you cannot speak mindfully about what you are trying to express, you can become passive or aggressive. Neither of these reactions is productive.

Cognitive reasons such as your self-perception, self-worth, and self-talk directly influence your ability to be assertive. Alberti and Emmons, the authors of *Your Perfect Right*, observed assertiveness helps to improve one's sense of self-worth. This is because it enables clear, open, and honest self-expression without worrying about how others may view or think about you. It lets you do this by overcoming any fear of judgement or lack of acceptance. When you are true to yourself, live the life you desire, and chase your goals, your self-worth improves. If you have a poor perception of yourself or your self-worth, your ability to be assertive diminishes. Assertiveness gives you the confidence to face different challenges and obstacles in life. When you confront and overcome a difficulty, your self-confidence improves. It is difficult to express what you want or desire without hesitation or fear if you do not value who you are.

Apart from self-worth, your self-esteem plays a significant role, too. If you consider your needs are worthless, or you are undeserving of anything good in life, or passive that your voice should be heard, then speaking up for yourself becomes problematic. As with cognitive factors, certain behaviours also act as barriers to assertiveness. The lack of self-care and indulging in negative thoughts about yourself will further reduce your self-esteem. Standing up for yourself becomes difficult when your self-esteem decreases and you start prioritizing everyone else before yourself. If you are engaging in any belittling thoughts, it can make you seem weak and indecisive. Quite simply, low self-esteem prevents you from acting in your own best interests.

Most tend to believe certain characteristics or traits are embryonically embedded within our psyche. When you start becoming rigid in your thinking, it becomes easier to believe you can do little to nothing to change the situation. This thought pattern stems from the belief that assertiveness is a character trait instead of a developed skill. This is a misconception. Anyone can learn to become assertive regardless of their current communication style.

If you take a moment and think about it, our self-worth, to a certain extent, is influenced by the roles we play in life or the status we hold in society. The problem with biases or societal conditioning is the great pressure it places on individuals to conform to these roles.

Social anxiety is a further barrier to assertiveness. This can prevent you from living your life. For instance, choosing to avoid interactions with others if there is a concern they will judge, criticize, or embarrass you. Or perhaps you do not want to be perceived as incompetent by others. Whatever the reason, if you are anxious about being yourself in social settings, how can you freely express your thoughts, opinions, or ideas? Fear prevents you from doing what you want. It is a lack of assertiveness can exacerbate social anxiety.

Your Journey

Are any of the barriers discussed in this chapter preventing you from becoming assertive? Identify what barriers you may face and brainstorm ways to overcome them. The road to assertiveness is to understand the different obstacles that stand in your way.

Chapter 4
Concentrate on Thinking Assertively

Do you know that your thoughts matter? They are the source of your perception and experience. If you have not given it any consideration, there is no time like the present to start examining what you are thinking. How you live and view your life depends on your thoughts. Our thoughts are nothing more than fleeting images created within our minds. These images do not have any inherent value associated with them unless we assign meaning to them. Similarly, these thoughts do not account for anything unless you act on them. Who is responsible for this? You are!

We are the authors of our thoughts. It is entirely up to you how seriously your thoughts need to be taken, how long they should be entertained, and their significance. This is one of the reasons why you need to start paying attention to them if you want to become assertive.

Public settings, social situations, professional surroundings, and close relationships are all different circumstances in life where you need to assert yourself. In these contexts, the lack of assertiveness can quickly pave the way for anxiety and fear-based thoughts. Fears are not only normal but a common part of the human psyche. If these fears and anxieties become a common part of your daily life, they will soon become problematic. Tackling fears and anxieties is easier said than done. I am speaking from personal experience here. Before saying or doing anything, I used to worry about what others would think. This constant worry soon transformed into an overpowering sense of anxiety, which prevented me from expressing myself. When I was learning to become assertive, I stumbled upon realizing that my fear and anxiety were holding me back.

A common concern that prevents assertiveness is the thought of disconnecting from others in your life. The idea of sabotaging relationships or disappointing our loved ones can induce fear and anxiety. A good technique to learn more about this is by taking a pen and paper and making a note of it. For two to three weeks, record whatever you feel each day. Over some time, chances are you will notice a pattern. Perhaps you experience anxiety whenever you need to say 'no.' Or maybe you struggle to have certain conversations with specific people in your life. Whenever you notice any fear or anxiety, note everything associated with it: the people around you, the scenario, where you are, and how you feel. Learning about your fear will give you the ammunition required to counter it.

Fear is a psychological manifestation of thoughts, ideas, or anything else that worries you. This tends to have related physiological effects, including increasing your heartbeat, rising blood pressure, and sweating. The best way to tackle your fear and reduce anxiety is by using the power of your imagination. Your mind is a potent weapon. Unless you learn how to control it, it will keep regulating your life. Your brain births all your fears and anxieties through your thoughts. If these fears result from your thinking, they can be transformed into something more positive. An effective practice is through visualization. For instance, if you are worried about disappointing your loved one for refusing a request, imagine a situation where it is resolved without unnecessary drama. Imagine you have politely explained you cannot help, asking what else you could do to support them, and simply ending the conversation. You can become assertive by shifting your brain to think about a positive outcome associated with an intimidating thought.

Once you have managed to get rid of your anxiety, it is time to regain control of your thoughts. The simplest way to do this is by concentrating on your breathing. Standing up for yourself may seem impossible when you are fearful or worried, especially if your thoughts are racing at 100 mph. When this happens, the physical symptoms of anxiety and fear will overwhelm you. When your body is stressed, it becomes increasingly difficult for your mind to calm down. Are you wondering what breathing has to do with all this? The next time you feel scared or worried, pay attention to your breathing. You will notice it becomes shallow and rapid. Now, pay attention to your breathing when you are happy and relaxed. By slowing down your breathing, you are slowing the racing thoughts, too. When your mind slows down, regaining control over your thoughts becomes easier. Standing up for yourself and becoming assertive will not seem as difficult when you are calmer and relaxed.

A simple breathing exercise is to close your eyes and breathe in for a count of four. As you count the numbers in your mind, keep inhaling—focus only on your breath and nothing else. Hold your breath for two seconds and breathe out for a count of four. As you count the numbers, exhale slowly. Breathe in, hold your breath, and breathe out. This is the pattern you need to repeat to complete one cycle. Repeat this simple exercise for 10-15 minutes, and you will automatically feel calmer.

Mindfulness is an active thinking activity designed to make you more aware of the present. Remember, anxieties are associated with thoughts of something that has already taken place or something that may or may not happen in the future. The best way to stop such anxiety-inducing thoughts is by returning your attention to the present. After all, the present is the only part of your life you have control over. The past cannot be changed, nor the future predicted. But how do you keep yourself in the present? By simply immersing yourself in an activity and forgetting about everything else. Perhaps you decide to spend some time planning your goals, reading a book, or possibly meeting a friend for coffee. This shift in concentration will make you more aware of what you are experiencing in the present and keep you there. It gives you better insight into your mind. When you do this, regulating your thoughts becomes easier.

If you want to think assertively, understand the attitude you maintain towards yourself. Unless you fix this first, you cannot work on the other things. It brings to mind a common safety precaution passengers are told before departing on a flight: In case of an emergency, put on your own oxygen mask before helping others. It can be quite tempting to help others first. Well, you need to stop doing this. Unless you help yourself first, you cannot help others. Remember, your thoughts are compelling: they shape how you perceive the world and influence your actions and behaviour.

Your Journey

Start paying attention to how you treat yourself. How you view yourself says a great deal about your self-worth. Do you accept who you are? Do you excessively criticize every move you make? Do you treat yourself with respect usually reserved for others? Do you feel guilty for prioritizing yourself? Do you usually ignore your needs while favouring others? Take some time for self-reflection and answer these questions. These questions can bring about some startling and rather unpleasant truths to the surface. However, you need to know the answer to these questions, or you cannot move forward.

As previously mentioned, unless you take control of your thoughts, it is not possible to change your life. Certain thoughts can harm your mind and prevent you from becoming assertive. Perhaps your inner critic says you cannot do something, or a toxic person discourages you from following your ambitions. These thoughts will reduce your assertiveness and diminish confidence in your abilities.

It is important to regulate your thoughts since they have the power of controlling your reality. Misleading thoughts result in a distorted sense of perspective. Irrespective of everything that is out of your control, your thoughts are always within your influence. Your thoughts are the by-products of your mind—and you have the power to regulate your mind and alter your thoughts.

When you learn to regulate your thinking, making better decisions becomes easier. It also helps you see yourself and life through a positive paradigm. Become aware of all your thoughts. This is the first step of identifying any negative thinking patterns. Whenever you notice a negative thought, name it. Rather than plunging into a vicious cycle of negativity, determine what the thought is actually about and question its origin. Do not simply accept it as the truth. Consider whether it is an opinion, fact, or a statement made by someone else. You may not have realized it, but most beliefs you harbour about yourself are not your own. More exactly, they are based on what you think others feel or have said about you. If you realize the negative thought is nothing more than someone else's opinion, what is the point in holding onto it? Start questioning your thoughts rather than believing them to be the ultimate truth.

Work on replacing negative thoughts with positive ones. In contrast to believing you can never get anything right, tell yourself you need to work on it a while longer. By simply tweaking how a sentence is framed, you can alter its meaning and change a negative sentence into a positive one. Using a mantra or phrase you can repeat whenever a negative thought enters your mind is also useful. Saying something as simple as "I am good enough" or "I can do it" will help.

Become mindful of all the thoughts you are thinking, and remember it is ultimately your choice. You have complete control over deciding whether you want to pay attention to a specific thought or not. The importance you give the thought is your decision.

Chapter 5
Overcoming People-Pleasing

Are you constantly trying hard to make everyone around you happy? Are you doing this at your own expense? If yes, you are a people-pleaser. You might say: What is wrong with pleasing people? It doesn't sound that bad, does it? The trouble is that people-pleasing is so much more than just simple acts of kindness. It involves altering and editing your words and behaviour to benefit someone else's reactions or feelings. It essentially refers to where you constantly go out of your way to do things for others because you believe it is what they want or need. You start giving up your own time and energy to cater to their needs. This incredible urge to please others can be quite damaging. If the sole purpose of your existence is to please others or you are constantly seeking external approval to feel better about yourself, it will reduce your self-esteem. If you want to be assertive, it is time to stop trying to please others all the time.

I constantly worried that others would not like me or be happy unless I gained their approval. I started associating my self-worth with what everyone around me seemed to believe or think. I spent so much time ruminating about what others were possibly thinking that I forgot about myself! Does this sound familiar to you? If yes, it is time to overcome your tendency to please people. Before you learn how to do this, it is important to understand why you do it.

No one likes to be rejected. This fear of rejection can be from someone else or even from a specific activity or task. You will avoid the person or task altogether if you believe that you will be snubbed regardless of what you do. For instance, if you fear dismissal from your job by displeasing your boss, you will go out of your way to keep them happy. Although it means the job is taking a toll on your mental health, you will ignore it as you do not want to lose your employment. Similarly, you may focus on pleasing your partner and agreeing with everything they say and do for fear of the relationship ending.

A common reason why people go along with what others say or do is to avoid conflict. If you fear confrontations, chances are you will go out of your way to keep the other person happy. However, by keeping everything bottled up, all the repressed emotions can essentially ruin the very relationship you were trying to save.

When I was in high school, I aspired to be part of a popular group of students. Sadly, it was not for reasons of intellectual advancement but rather their trendy and 'with-it' reputation, which other students in the school admired. I was willing to do practically anything to be a member of this elite club. Whether it was following the latest fashion, listening to music I did not enjoy, or readily accepting their views and opinions, I was prepared to do whatever it would take to fit in. This is one of the most common reasons for people-pleasing. It is a human tendency to seek the feeling of belongingness. The real trouble starts when you start ignoring your true self while chasing such desires.

In the previous section, it was discussed that the fear of disappointing others would prevent assertiveness. No one wants to let down the people in our lives, especially those we love. At the same time, it is also difficult to please everyone. This fear of disappointing others can prevent you from living your life. Keep in mind no matter how much effort is exerted, it is impossible to please everyone. But remember, you are not responsible for what others think or feel either. Saying 'no' is a life skill that many people struggle to overcome. The inability to say 'no' usually stems from a lack of boundaries. If you do not have any limits, others will take you for granted. Most are fearful of declining requests as they do not want to hurt others or are unsure how to do it effectively.

The inability to say 'no' in the workplace, for example, means you are constantly stuck with additional responsibilities that can leave you overworked and stressed. Assertiveness is crucial for your overall productivity and efficiency. Whether you are an employee or an employer, you cannot achieve professional success without it. It is the ability to express your ideas, thoughts, and opinions without worrying about others' responses. This, in turn, leads to greater self-esteem and self-confidence. Effective communication is the ability to become a good listener, acknowledge differing views, and standing your ground without violating others' rights.

Research suggests assertiveness positively affects one's overall sense of well-being (Maryam Paeezy et al., 2010). It gives you the inner courage needed to express yourself openly and honestly in social settings. When you feel confident about yourself and have healthy self-esteem, social interactions become easier. Assertiveness can reduce social anxiety rather than finding these situations stressful (Raziyeh Saeed Manesh et al., 2015). It has other benefits, too. Ahmad Ali Eslami et al. (2016) determined that assertiveness can reduce stress, depression, and anxiety. Dr Valliammal Shanmugam and Dr B. V. Kathyayini's research (2017) suggests it increases self-esteem. It is a combination of these factors that contribute towards a positive attitude of life.

Your Journey

Take a moment to reflect on the preceding list of benefits. How can each one be incorporated into your life? Which benefits do you connect with the most and want to develop immediately? Which benefits do you think will be a challenge?

According to Daniel Ames (2009), the need to strike a balance between low and high levels of assertiveness at work is crucial for efficiency and productivity. This may prevent you from asking for new opportunities at work, impeding you from going after what you desire and essentially hampering your professional growth. It could also make others believe they can take you for granted. When this happens, you cannot function at your optimum level. As with low levels of assertiveness, high levels of assertiveness are also problematic. There is a fine line to tread between assertiveness and aggression. If you become too assertive, it can come across as aggressive, dominating, and arrogant. Remember, assertiveness is asking for what you want without violating others' rights. Demanding what you want, regardless of others, is aggressiveness. Aggression will not get you far in life. It is counter-productive to success. Balance is the universal law of nature. Without balance, all functions cease to exist. Never forget this in any aspect of life.

If people easily influence you, chances are you strive to be more like them. For instance, if you are drawn to a public figure, you will most likely listen and follow their every word without giving them any conscious thought. Similarly, if your self-worth is based on external validation, you will be quick to help others all the time but are not there for yourself. For example, suppose your self-worth is solely dependent on external sources, such as getting likes on social media or any compliments you receive. In such circumstances, you will probably continue to make sacrifices to please others. The problem with all this is your sense of self is taken away. When this happens, you live your life trying to make everyone happy, but it will only make you miserable over time.

When you make someone happy or gain their approval, you feel better about yourself, albeit momentarily. It sounds like a logical way to go through life. It seems like the perfect path you can walk, following it for years, believing it reduces anxiety associated with disapproval. It is viewed as an ideal way of making others like you in the sense of not doing anything that will earn their displeasure whilst enjoying little pats on your back every once in a while. Unfortunately, there will come a time when this constant need of seeking approval will run its course. The behaviour that made you feel pretty good about yourself will become problematic. You start living a life you do not want but persist as others begin to expect it. Rather than living life on your terms and dreaming the dreams you desire, you start living your life on the back of the expectations of others. You stop taking any chances because you do not want to be frowned on. You do what everyone wants and expect their approval in return. There is nothing wrong with seeking approval. The only problem is it should never come at your own expense. If the urge to seek external validation prevents you from living your own life or doing what you truly want, it does not serve any purpose.

Approval-seeking is effectively holding you back from being your true self. Perhaps you have never even realized it, but your efficiency reduces due to this excessive need for validation. There is a possibility of avoiding things that feel important to you, an anxiousness about trying activities outside your comfort zone or constantly worrying about what others say or expect of you. All this prevents exploring potential opportunities in life. If you are too apprehensive to believe in yourself and start thinking your performance can never be perfect, it can get to a point where you are so worried about failure that you do not even take the first step.

This is one of the reasons why it is important to let go of this need for approval. Regardless of whether you are a high achiever or not, attaining positive results that others expect at your own cost does not serve any purpose. If you are driven to impress others or seek validation, it will not add value to your life. People-pleasing will leave you feeling overworked, tired, and disconnected from your true self.

To cut loose of this need for acceptance, you must understand yourself. If all your decisions are based on others' approval, you will lose your sense of self-awareness. The best way to break free of this cycle is by understanding what is important to you, the factors that drive you, and things that make you happy. Why are you doing it if you feel stuck with work you do not enjoy, find it meaningless, or adds no value to your life? If you engage in any habit that is not in sync with what you feel, you are not true to yourself. Start focusing your time and energy on getting in touch with what matters to you. Take some time and answer these questions:

- What thoughts keep you awake at night?
- How do you like to spend your time?
- What matters to you in life?
- Is there something you truly value?

By answering these questions, you will better understand your values, principles, and goals. To increase your self-awareness, you need to take small daily steps. Rather than making your decisions based on others' thoughts, settle on what is right for you. Become conscious of the choices available to you and do what feels right. Try to understand the simple fact that you are not responsible for others. You are not answerable for how they feel, and you certainly are not accountable for what they think. The only person you are responsible for is you.

When you are aware of your priorities and values, it becomes easier to establish boundaries. It also gives you a better sense of all the resources available at your disposal. Setting priorities helps us understand the best use of these limited resources and is a great way of knowing when you are comfortable saying 'yes' or 'no.' It helps you recognize what is most important to you. If all your time and energy is spent on activities that do not add any value to your life or hold little to no meaning, you will be left feeling frustrated and unfulfilled. To avoid all this, start establishing priorities in every aspect of your life.

Remember, you always have a choice. Unless you consciously give this away, no one can impose their will on you. The entitlement to choose is our inherent right, and do not let anyone tell you otherwise. Whatever you may have believed until now, it is essential to understand you have the choice to say 'yes' or 'no' in any situation.

Whenever anyone asks you for a favour, rather than readily saying 'yes,' tell them you need some time to think about it. It is perfectly fine to stall. When you do this, you have some space to decide whether the commitment is something you can work with or not. It is also an opportunity to ask for additional details before agreeing to the request. Consider the time, effort, energy, and resources needed for completing the task. By stalling for a while, you are essentially giving yourself a way out!

There will always be people who will try to take advantage of you. It is important to be on your guard for flatterers and manipulators. Are you wondering how you can spot such people? They are the ones who use flattery or praise to exploit others. Let us assume you are a good baker. An acquaintance contacts you, praises your baking skills, then sneaks in an order. By the time you realize what has happened, you are already complying with the request. If you want to avoid this, you must become conscious of those around you. Become aware of your conversations and pay extra attention to what others say.

If you do not want to deny the request, setting time limits is an efficient way to become assertive. If you have decided to help someone, let them know the time of day that works for you and how long you can give them. For example, if your colleague asks for help with their presentation, explain that you need to complete the task you are working on, but you can help them for 20-30 minutes when you are finished. This lets the other person know you cannot be taken for granted.

Creating a mantra is an effective way to avoid readily accepting a request. For instance, repeating, "I have a choice, and I can say no," can be helpful when a certain person who always manages to talk you into something is heading your way. This mantra will act as a reminder to not give in to the urge to please others at your own expense.

Assertiveness is all about developing a connection. A simple way to do this is by practicing empathy. For instance, if you are having a conversation with a friend, empathetic assertion means placing yourself in their shoes to understand their position but acknowledging you may not be able to help them. This satisfies the basic human need to be listened to and understood. Your friend should not be upset if they know you empathize with them.

Standing up for yourself, respecting your boundaries, and understanding your individuality are all associated with the ability to say 'no.' When refusing a request, it is important to decline the request with conviction. After all, you need to have confidence in what you are saying if you want others to believe you! If you have no faith in what you are saying, you will never be heard. If you are struggling to say 'no,' remind yourself of all the benefits associated with this action. For instance, the time saved can be used to rest, spend time with friends and family, or pursue leisure activities. Or perhaps you are already stressed with work and do not need any other additional responsibilities.

Whenever you express your opinions, be sure not to make any excuses—you do not have to justify yourself to others. There is always a temptation of defending your decision. However, the minute you start explaining yourself in any detail, you are essentially giving others wiggle room. Rather than a sharp 'no,' you can briefly describe your reasons and offer an alternative solution, but do not engage in any lengthy dialogue. For example, my friend required transportation to the railway station at 11.30 am one weekday morning, but I could not oblige. I said something along the lines of, "I would really like to help, but I have a doctor's appointment at 11.00 am, and I do not want to commit to taking you to the station in the event I make you late for your train. However, I'm going into town at 10.00 am and would be pleased to take you to the station, if that wouldn't be too early for you? Otherwise, I will have to say no on this occasion."

It's a different dynamic in the work environment, of course, and saying 'no' to taking on additional responsibilities is not easy. Again, explaining in detail why you cannot do something does not serve any purpose; it only gives others a chance to suggest different ways to accommodate them! For example, say a manager allocates their subordinate a new project. At the time, they are already under pressure with several deadlines looming. The new project would overstretch their workload capacity, affecting both the quality of their work and the ability to meet the timescales. The increased workload is simply not viable. Their response could be, "It's a project I would really like to be involved with. However, I do not have the time available to give it my all. I have a report to complete for the Board of Directors next week. Then I need to compile and present the sales figures for the end of the second quarter and negotiate new contracts with our suppliers over the next two weeks. It's a project I am keen to be involved with, but if you want me to take it on, I will need you to help me reprioritise my work and renegotiate the existing timescales." In this instance, let us assume the manager understands they cannot delegate the subordinate's current work commitments. With the new project requiring an immediate start date, they assign it to another colleague. Now, what would have happened if the subordinate did not dare to say 'no'? Well, certainly, they would have put themself under enormous stress, timescales would have slipped, they would have been less productive, and the quality of their work would have suffered. The diminishment in their performance would leave them open to criticism from various parts of the organization. This is a prime example of why assertiveness is so important.

There is a time and a place for assertiveness. Whenever you are asserting yourself, ask the question, "Is this worth it?" Learning to decide when to stand up for yourself and when to let go of certain things is important in all aspects of life.

We all have physical limits, and this is equally true of our mental and emotional boundaries. If you constantly push yourself beyond them, you will become burnt out. These limits are the primary reason why establishing and maintaining boundaries is important for your overall health. The simplest way to develop these limits is by understanding what you can and are willing to do. After this, you need to stop. When it comes to boundaries, you must clearly communicate what they are and the purpose they serve.

If someone fails to respect your boundaries, it means they do not care for you. If they accept you for who you are, they will understand your limits. A person who values you will never expect to push past the boundaries you have set. For instance, let us assume you have a specific friend who calls you only in a time of need and expects you to support them through their emotional difficulties. However, when things are going well, you never hear from them. The conversations always end up making you despondent whilst they feel better about themselves. This is a very one-sided relationship, and there is no reason why you need to be miserable to make someone else feel better—draw a line and stand by it. Unless you take care of yourself, you cannot help others.

The worry of losing friends, social circle, or any relationships in life is present in everyone. The only thing that differs is the degree to which it affects your life. If you are constantly saying and doing something because of this worry, you are not true to others or yourself. It is time to ask, "Why do I believe a fallout will be a catastrophe?" This may seem like a rather difficult question, but it is an important one. If this is all true for you, it is time to change. Rather than worrying about a fallout, ask yourself what terrifies you about it? To begin with, you may realize that others do not think about you to the extent you originally believed. I no longer worry about ridding myself of any undesirable associations. If others stop responding to you or treat you differently after asserting yourself, it is an unhealthy relationship. If your bonds are solid, the people in your life will understand what you are saying and your reasons.

Using positive self-talk is a useful way to let go of the dire need for external approval. Do not expect others to be caring towards you unless you are kind to yourself. If you are struggling with any negative thoughts, either replace them with positive ones or reframe them. A little self-soothing can instantly calm you, making it easier to think more clearly and reduce any negative self-talk.

There is absolutely no way in which you can satisfy the wants and needs of everyone you meet. Yes, you can make someone happy, but remember, it will always be temporary. Try to understand that true happiness always starts from within. When this happens, no one else can take it away. Unfortunately, most people do not realize this and needlessly spend their time and energy trying to keep others happy. Start by positively changing your own life. You have the power to change your thoughts and feelings. You can change them for better or worse, and the choice is yours. Once you realize true happiness is within your reach, it will change your perception of the world in general.

Your Journey

Take a moment and reflect on the ways to avoid people-pleasing. Which ones can you apply to your life immediately? Which ones would best serve you at work? At home? With friends? Make a list of actions you plan to take to prevent people-pleasing behaviours.

Chapter 6
Start Understanding Yourself

Understanding yourself is an essential aspect of becoming assertive. How can you be decisive if you do not know what you are standing up for? How can you confidently express your wants and needs if you do not know what they are? How can you live your life assertively if you do not understand what you are trying to achieve? How can you establish your boundaries if you are not aware of where to draw the line? The only way to answer these questions is by understanding your beliefs and values.

Any idea that you hold as the truth is known as a belief. Beliefs can be enabling and limiting and are formed from personal experiences, experiments, societal or cultural norms, and others' opinions. When a belief becomes a part of our system, we try to defend it and live our lives by it. They usually guide our response to situations and enable our decisions. For instance, an enabling belief is understanding our positive attributes, such as courage, knowledge, skills, and so on. Believing we are weak, incapable of succeeding, or simply boring are examples of limiting beliefs.

Values are long-lasting beliefs about things that are important to you. They are the standards you use to live your life and make decisions. A belief turns into a value when your commitment to it grows, and you associate a great deal of importance with it. Values can also be the goals that motivate your actions and act as the guiding principles for living your life. We all have different values influenced by our upbringing, culture, life experiences, and other external factors.

Now you know the meaning of beliefs and their importance, it is time to identify them. You may not have realized that negative core beliefs can be running in the background of your mind. It is easy to think you are aware of all the words you say—this is partially true. In reality, it is quite likely you have never paid any attention to the deeper meanings embedded within the words you speak. Most words are usually an automatic response to our belief system. By becoming aware of your words, it becomes easier to identify your beliefs. For instance, you may tell someone, "I was late to work due to the traffic, and it's so frustrating." This can seem like a random sentence that talks about the terrible traffic situation. Now, pay close attention to it. You are letting your emotions be governed by an external event that is clearly beyond your control. You are looking for something outside that can be blamed for the unpleasant emotions you are experiencing. How many times have you said, "so and so's behaviour upsets me," or "that person makes me feel…"? Do you see what is happening here? As with the traffic example, this shows how our reactions affect our words.

Our minds are designed to avoid all sorts of unpleasantness. Perhaps someone's behaviour is upsetting to you because it clashes with one of your core beliefs. For example, if you believe every relationship is an equal partnership, everything you think about relationships will be based on this belief. Now, if your partner does not help with any chores at home, their behaviour is against your belief. This is the primary reason why their behaviour upsets you. By paying a little extra attention to what you say, you can identify your core beliefs.

Start paying attention to the emotions you experience. Identifying an emotion makes it easier to find the belief behind it. Let us assume that you fear talking in front of an audience. Immediately before delivering an important speech at a conference, you have an anxiety attack. The anxiety you experience is the result of a specific emotion you are experiencing – worry. However, what is causing this worry? After a little self-reflection, you realize you are concerned about disappointing the audience. By identifying the emotion, it becomes easier to understand your belief. Before the event has occurred, you have already created a thought that the audience will be disappointed. Do you see the problem in this example? By believing you will disappoint the audience, you have assumed responsibility for others' feelings. How can you possibly be responsible for what others feel? By accepting this responsibility, you are increasing your stress and anxiety!

Your life experiences tend to influence your core values. These are the beliefs that affect how you live your life. Some common examples of core values include:

- Friendship.
- Achievement.
- Enthusiasm.

- Creativity.
- Ambition.
- Fun.
- Growth.
- Happiness.
- Health.
- Joy.
- Intelligence.
- Loyalty.
- Passion.
- Resilience.

The list is seemingly endless. A quick search on the Internet will display a result of all the possible values you can hold. Go through this list of values and determine whether they resonate with you or not. If something chimes with you, make a note of it. If not, take some time for self-reflection and consider all the different values that hold meaning to you. Usually, the values we live by are personified in those we love and admire. If you take a moment and think about it, it makes perfect sense. What do you love about your best friend? What do you love about your parents? Start asking yourself this question while going through a list of people you love, admire, or value as role models. For instance, you probably admire your parents because of their resilience, relentless dedication, empathy, and ability to love unconditionally. These are all personal values they possess that you respect.

Now, consider your life experiences. Reflect upon some of the best and worst experiences you have encountered. Whether winning a race at school or your first heartbreak, each significant life experience teaches you something about yourself. For instance, your breakup may have taught you that certain values, such as honesty and loyalty, are important to you. Now that you have a long list of values, it is time to review and categorize them. For example, values such as honesty, passion, love, and loyalty can be grouped together as those most important for your relationships. After you have completed this step, chances are you will realize you have several core values. Now, place in order your top core values. In every category, identify one or two core values that are more important than others. Ideally, it is suggested that you should not have more than five to ten core values. If you have more than ten core values, ask yourself, "What are the essential values?" Even if you have listed twenty core values and believe they are all important, give yourself some time to notice those you pay more attention to; these are your top core values. These values should be used as the basic guidelines in living your life and making decisions.

Usually, fears and anxieties are worse in our heads than they are in reality. To become assertive, you must challenge your thinking. The best way to go about it is by writing it down. A journal helps identify unhelpful or unassertive thoughts. Irrespective of what you are dealing with, set aside fifteen to twenty minutes daily for journaling. Think of it as a brain dump. While writing, the only thing you must remember is to let your thoughts flow. You do not have to judge any words you have written or worry about their meaning. You can do all of that later. For now, the only thing to do is to keep writing. Maintain this journal for two weeks and at the end of this period, read through all the entries. Going through everything you have written then becomes easier to make sense of any thoughts that are bothering you. When you start reading what you have written, you can discover hidden patterns or thoughts guiding your mind. By giving yourself a break and reading what you have written later, you essentially view your thoughts from a different viewpoint. The shift in perspective makes it easier to identify your beliefs.

Let us assume you asked a friend to meet you at the cinema, and they said 'no.' The first step is to describe the situation and state the facts. If this situation unfolded like a movie, how would you describe it? Simply write down what you asked and the reply received. The next step is to identify the emotion you are experiencing. Ask yourself the following questions to determine your emotion: What am I feeling right now? Am I feeling more than one emotion? If yes, what are they? What is the intensity of this emotion? Then rate the intensity of the emotion on a scale of 1-100. If you are feeling multiple emotions, they do not have to add up to 100. Every emotion must be rated individually on a scale of 0-100, ranging from zero to maximum intensity. Once you have rated your emotion, identify any physical symptoms you experienced and your behaviour, asking yourself what you experienced in your body and how you reacted to the situation. The next step is to classify your thoughts. These thoughts can be in the form of values, your interpretation of the situation, any assumptions, or even pre-existing beliefs. At times, your thoughts may also be in the form of images or pictures rather than words.

Now, let us go back to the example. Your friend said 'no' when you invited them to the cinema. Using the method outlined above, we shall apply it to this situation: The first step is to state the facts. Say, during a previous telephone conversation, you both agreed to meet up at the cinema on a certain evening. Your friend then reneged on their promise without giving a reasonable explanation. The emotion you may be experiencing is anger that you turned down other engagements to keep the date free, and now there is a void in your evening plans. Let us assume you then refused to answer their further messages or phone calls. This is your behavioural response to the situation. The thought that may be going through your head is they no longer value the relationship to the same extent you do and would prefer to spend their recreation time doing something else.

Once you have completed these steps, the next part of the exercise is to rate the strength of your beliefs. In the above example, the belief that took shape is that your friend no longer values your relationship to the same extent as you do. This is a belief stemming from your thoughts. Rate your belief on a scale of 0-100, with zero representing you do not believe the thought and one hundred being absolute belief in the thought. Once you have all this information in place, the next step is to dispute the thought. There is no reason to believe whatever you think is the indisputable truth or a fact. So, rather than allowing unhelpful thoughts to manifest as strong beliefs, it is time to challenge them. Here are some questions you can use to dispute the belief:

- Is my thought aggressive, passive, or assertive?
- Was my response to the situation aggressive, passive, or assertive?
- Is there any evidence supporting my thought?
- Is there any proof invalidating my thought?
- Am I violating someone else's rights or my rights in this situation?
- Can I view this situation from a different perspective?
- Is there any other possible way to interpret this situation?

Asking yourself these questions essentially halts and changes your thought process. Rather than assuming the worst about yourself, others, and the situation, you can carefully process what has happened. It helps infuse your thoughts with positivity and assertiveness. The final step is to revisit your emotional intensity. In light of the thought evaluation process, ask yourself whether the emotional intensity you experienced is actually appropriate for the situation. Be honest with yourself while completing this exercise. Chances are, once you carefully analyse your thoughts, you will realize things are worse in your head than in reality. If you keep practicing this exercise, it will reduce the intensity of your emotions, help regain control over your thoughts, and lead you to become more assertive.

Your Journey

How can you rephrase some of your thoughts to allow yourself to think more productively? Take a moment to come up with some mantras, affirmations, or phrases you can use to reframe your thoughts.

Journaling is useful in other aspects of developing your assertiveness. It is quite easy to concentrate on everything that goes wrong. It is a human tendency to be highly critical of ourselves and focus on our failures. The best way to counteract this tendency is to write down all the situations where you have shown some assertiveness and achieved little wins. The idea is when you succeed, do not forget to celebrate it. If you do not hesitate to criticize yourself, do not be reluctant to celebrate your victories! This is a way of showing self-appreciation. By acknowledging everything you do well, you are slowly building your ability to be assertive. The idea behind this activity is to feel much more relaxed and calm your mind. When you can do this, letting go of negative thoughts becomes easier.

Chapter 7
How to Assert Your Opinions, Ideas, and Desires

Learning to become assertive can seem a little overwhelming, and it is always better to take small steps. For instance, if you have a specific idea or an opinion you want to share with a group but are worried about what others may think, why not voice it to a family member or a friend for their comment? Receiving credible feedback from trustworthy sources increases your confidence. Start looking for different occasions to become more comfortable expressing your feelings. Begin by talking about your ideas, opinions, or views in a smaller setting. Alternatively, you can bring to mind your past experiences and develop from there. For example, think about a specific situation in the past where you failed to express yourself, and then ask what you would do differently in the same scenario? The next time a similar situation presents itself, you can use this newfound insight to articulate your views.

Similarly, another suggestion is to visualize the conversation you want with another person. By visualizing a discussion in your mind, you have an opportunity to prepare a script for what you want to say and how to say it. When you know how you will convey your opinions or ideas, implementing them later becomes easier. It also allows you to analyze any potential questions or misgivings others may raise. By preparing yourself for the conversation, you are reducing any chances of surprise. This action increases positive thinking and reduces any doubts you may experience. Stand in front of a mirror and practice what you want to say. While doing this, pay attention to your body language, including facial expressions. If your words contradict your body language, it can send a confusing message. Try saying "Thank you" with a smile on your face and then whilst frowning. The former sounds sincere, whereas the latter sounds sarcastic or artificial. When rehearsing your behaviour, you may notice your body language is defensive even when it is not your intention. This gives you a chance to practice what you want to say and ensuring your words and body language are in tune with each other.

You may not have given it any conscious thought until now, but small voices have significant impacts. Why is it important that you overcome your nerves? Are you helping anyone else by speaking your mind? How are you helping others? Is there anyone you can inspire by doing this? Will you be satisfied with yourself by speaking up? What are the consequences of not asserting your opinion? Have this simple conversation with yourself, and it becomes easier to determine what you stand to gain from it.

A common reason why most struggle with assertiveness is that they need to feel confident before they can communicate effectively. Remember, you do not necessarily have to feel confident before you act. Usually, it is the other way around.

Stop waiting for the right moment or until you are ready. Take action!

When you are communicating, ensure you stick to the facts. This is especially true whenever you are expressing any beliefs, opinions, or ideas. Do not let your emotions enter the conversation. Once emotions overrule the conversation, logic usually takes a back seat. Logic, rational thinking, and facts should be at the front of your mind if you want to convey assertiveness. When you present hard facts and solid reasoning, refuting an idea becomes difficult. It also initiates a positive conversation and dialogue about the ideas you are suggesting. Presenting facts makes your information more credible, thoughtful, and well laid out. These are simple things that inspire confidence.

Always pay attention to your body language. It conveys more than the words you speak. Whether it is a frown, smile, or grin, different expressions convey different emotions. Whenever you are communicating, ensure your verbal and non-verbal communication is in synchronization. If you are saying one thing, but your expressions convey something else, it creates ambiguity and reduces the trust others feel in you. If you want to portray confidence, ensure your body language is on point.

Have you ever heard the phrase, 'Fake it 'til you make it'? In a nutshell, it means giving the impression you are self-assured even when you lack knowledge in a subject area or whilst learning a new skill. Take on the role of a confident persona and see the difference it makes to your conversations with others. To do this, find someone who inspires you. This could be a friend, family member, or public figure. Then start mimicking their qualities. Begin in a safe space, such as with your friends or loved ones. Chances are, you will receive positive reactions, which will increase your desire to develop the positive habit of growing confidence. If you begin to have doubts, ask yourself what the person you are emulating would do if they were in your situation. Use the answer to this question to display your confidence to others.

Whenever you are sharing your opinion, stop worrying about the outcome. This is one point most people fail to consider. Some let their voices go unheard because they are concerned about the upshot. For instance, you may shy away from expressing an idea about a project at work because you are worried about others judging you. Perhaps you are concerned others will think your ideas are foolish or silly. You may like to believe everyone is constantly paying attention to what you are saying and doing, but it is hardly the truth in reality. If others are dismissive or try to put you down, do not react to the situation. Rather reassert your opinions in a confident manner backed up by strong facts and logic. Do not be afraid of expressing yourself.

There will be instances when you come across non-assertive people. If you are working on becoming more assertive yourself, standing up for others can develop your skill. If you see a colleague at work who is quite hesitant and shy about sharing their ideas, why not prompt them? By advocating for others who have a tough time communicating their views, you are also working on your own assertiveness. A simple statement such as, "I believe so and so has a good idea," will do the trick. Standing up for others is a great feel-good factor knowing you are helping someone and adding value to their life. Use this positive feeling as a motivation to become more assertive.

If you are struggling to express your views, ideas, or desires, then concentrate on the underlying reason why you need to do this. For instance, if it is a professional setting, you bring value and expertise to the table. In a personal relationship, the idea of asserting your thoughts and opinions can strengthen the relationship or reduce any misunderstandings. By focusing on your 'why' will give you renewed confidence.

Chapter 8
What to Do When You Do Not Agree with Others

No two people are truly exactly alike. It is not only difficult but near impossible to find someone who agrees with everything you say and do. You will find like-minded people, but a difference in opinion is not only common but should be expected. Whether it is your professional or personal life, there will be disagreements. You will never find an environment where everyone agrees with each other all the time—it is simply not possible.

An important part of becoming an assertive communicator is to understand it is perfectly normal to disagree. Disagreements are not a sign of weak relationships. The only thing that harms any relationship is how you deal with those divergences. Differences are bound to crop up sooner or later. The decision to positively embrace such discord entirely depends on you.

Disagreements can quickly spiral into arguments and escalate into relationship-ending conversations. The primary reason why differences crop up is that we fail to understand each other. If you are too busy trying to make yourself heard or others refuse to listen, you cannot have an effective conversation. Everyone in a conversation needs to shift between the roles of speaker and listener for it to be effective.

The simple point you need to understand is we are all different. That said, we are also more alike than you probably realized. After all, we all want to be listened to, respected, appreciated and acknowledged. These are similarities we share despite our differences. By understanding that we are all unique, it becomes easier to appreciate varying points of view. Acceptance is not synonymous with an agreement—you can appreciate someone even when you do not agree.

By understanding the other person's viewpoint and paying attention to their position, handling disagreements and reducing the scope of further escalation becomes much easier. You cannot identify with the other person if you do not keep an open mind. This essentially means learning to rid yourself of any biases, preconceived notions, or pre-formed conclusions about what the other person is saying. To be more precise, you are actively and objectively listening to whatever they are saying and seeking to understand their position. This is the only way to have mature and honest conversations. Unless you keep an open mind about what the other person is saying, you cannot truly understand what others are trying to convey.

Whenever you are dealing with any disagreements, it is important to look past your triggers. If you are triggered by something someone said, it can result in a confrontation. Avoid comparing what is happening right now with whatever may have occurred in the past. You cannot change the past, but you can learn your lessons and move on. Once you decide to move on, you need to concentrate on the present and nothing else.

It is easy to blame, accuse, or make excuses for your feelings and emotions, especially in heated disagreements. It must be understood that you are the only one responsible for what or how you feel. It is quite simple to say, "You made me angry." However, understand that your anger is something within your control. All the emotions you are experiencing are your own. You need to take responsibility for your feelings. Unless you do this, you cannot move forward in a conversation.

If you do not agree with what someone else is saying, it does not give you the right to disrupt them. If you dislike interruption when you are speaking, then you should be equally respectful towards others. There is no harm in becoming a good listener. Perhaps all you need to do is listen to what the other person says to understand their perspective. This also increases the motivation of the other person to hear what you have to say.

Whatever you do, you must not resort to negative language in any form. Personal insults, sarcastic remarks, or anything else along these lines is undesirable. There is no reason why you should use negative language. No one wants to be called out or hear all the bad things they have done in the past. If you are trying to hurt the other person to shut them down, stop yourself. When dealing with someone you do not agree with, ask yourself what you will achieve by being negative towards them? In all likelihood, you will get nothing out of it. If you can add something positive to whatever you are saying, there is an increased possibility of others listening to you.

Disagreements are a part of life. Learning to deal with them effectively is the only thing that makes the difference between a happy or a miserable existence.

It is perfectly okay to agree to disagree. It may sound like a cliché, but this is quite true. As mentioned, no two individuals are alike, and there will be topics you can never agree on. If it feels like the discussion has reached a moot point where neither party is willing to shift their position, what is the point in haranguing each other? It is better to end the conversation and simply move on. Learning to walk away is equally as important as starting a conversation. When you agree to disagree, it does not mean you are wrong and the other person is right. Every conversation is not about winning. Disagreements are inevitable, and there is nothing wrong with it. However, there is a right and a wrong way to present your arguments. Once you walk away from a disagreement, let it stay in the past. Do not bring up past confrontations or issues when discussing present disputes. Bringing up the past does not serve any purpose except opening old wounds. Learn your lessons and move on. Certain things are a given in life, including disagreements in relationships. By choosing to handle them with a positive mindset can make all the difference.

Chapter 9
Rules About Feedback

Whenever you are giving feedback, you need to communicate it with confidence and without any ambiguity. Assertiveness helps convey your message clearly and respectfully to the other person. In contrast, plenty of grace is required while receiving any form of feedback. From keeping your emotions in check to staying calm and asking for clarification, several techniques are available to make more sense of the criticism. In the end, assertiveness is a helpful skill that is about communication and the relationship you share with others.

Whenever you are giving any positive feedback, ensure it is thoughtful. Have you ever been complimented for something specific in your life? Chances are you still remember the compliment. Why does this happen? Whenever others praise us, we feel appreciated, acknowledged, and understood. It creates a sense of validation. These are all positive feelings. Positive feedback will make the receiver feel motivated, engaged, and more focused on whatever they do.

You do not have to praise others for the sake of it. Do not offer any compliments unless you truly mean what you are saying. You do not have to flatter anyone. There is nothing to gain by being fake. If there is something specific someone else has done, praise them for it. Genuine feedback can be quite uplifting and motivating. Remember the different aspects of assertiveness mentioned earlier? One of the most important parts of being assertive is to communicate honestly, directly, and openly. Another tip you should remember while giving positive feedback is your body language. Maintain eye contact, use appropriate facial expressions, stick to basic hand gestures, and do not forget to smile. While giving positive feedback, ensure it is specific. Telling your subordinates they are an excellent employee is positive feedback, but it is also vague. Is there something specific they do that makes them an exceptional employee? Or perhaps there is a particular skill they possess that sets them apart from others. Saying, "I admire your punctuality," is better than "You are an excellent employee." Unless you are specific in what you are praising, the positive feedback will not amount to much.

There is no point in praising someone long after the event has occurred. For instance, praising them after the meeting makes sense if your team member did exceptionally well during a specific client meeting. It does not make any sense if you bring it up two months later. Chances are, the other person does not even remember it. If the feedback is not timely, it tends to diminish their accomplishments. After all, you do not want the other person to feel like their efforts are going unnoticed—that is not a good feeling. Whenever you give any positive feedback, even if it is a small compliment, ensure you concentrate only on their efforts. This helps create a growth mindset in the receiver. When you focus on their effort, it shows you care. If you focus purely on results, it creates negative reinforcement. Others will start believing they will only be praised when they accomplish the results you desire. This is an unhealthy attitude.

It may sound a little surprising, but gracefully accepting praise is also a skill. Many find it difficult to internalize any feedback they receive, especially if they already struggle with assertiveness. If you do not believe in your skills or have low self-confidence, accepting praise becomes difficult. This difficulty further increases if you do not think you deserve to be appreciated. Negative thinking can prevent you from fully receiving positive feedback. The first step of receiving positive feedback is to accept the praise. Do not deflect it, and do not minimize your achievement. You do not have to brush it away by saying, "It was nothing," or "Anyone could do it." You may not have realized, but the inability to accept praise reflects poorly on you. It shows you do not believe in yourself, which is why you cannot digest the recognition given. If someone is complimenting you, it is because you are good at what you do. So, accept the praise. Whenever you receive any positive feedback, say "Thank you." While receiving the recognition, ensure you do not let it go to your head. Praise can improve your self-confidence and self-esteem. At the same time, do not let these important traits become dependent on the recognition received. If you seek endorsement, you will become a people-pleaser and depend on external validation to feel better. Simply start to believe in yourself and your abilities while learning to accept all types of feedback.

Do not blindly accept praise. Receiving positive feedback may not be easy for you, but taking compliments without understanding them does not serve any purpose. The idea of feedback is always to start a conversation. If someone praises your skills, talent, or even specific characteristics, acknowledge them. Once you have acknowledged and accepted the praise, ask some follow-up questions. If your efforts at work are recognized, ask what aspect of your actions they appreciated. Perhaps you did something specific, or maybe the approach you used was the reason for the praise received. Unless you understand the feedback, it will become difficult to repeat such behaviour in the future. Whenever you are receiving any positive comments, it is important to be a good listener. Pay careful attention to the answers you receive. If someone conveys what you do well or something they appreciate about you, listen attentively to the comments. Use this information to your advantage in the future. How you view yourself will be quite different from how others view you. The positive feedback you have received can be used for your journey of self-discovery. Chances are you have never paid any attention to them before. When you look at yourself from a different perspective, your self-image changes. By asking specific questions and becoming a good listener, you can understand what differentiates you from others.

Giving negative feedback can sound quite simple; after all, how hard can it be to tell someone what they are doing wrong? Unfortunately, it is usually never straightforward. While giving negative feedback, it is important to remember not to demotivate the other person. At the same time, the feedback should not backfire. Since honest communication is an important aspect of assertiveness, learning to give negative feedback is essential in personal and professional environments. Before you provide any feedback, it is important to understand it should come from a place of care and consideration. You are giving negative feedback because you care about the other person. If this primary element is absent, you are not giving negative feedback for the right reasons. The idea of negative feedback is to help the other person fix certain issues they are probably unaware of. For instance, at work, you will undoubtedly care that a project is successful, the team are making progress, or your teammate's development is moving in the right direction. These are all objectives showing your care and consideration for the receiver. It is now important to let the receiver know this. How can you let the receiver know whatever you are about to say is not a personal insult? Something along the lines of, "I am not criticizing you as a person," "I want to see you succeed," or "I care for your growth and development" will do. This shows the criticism is meant to be helpful.

Often we can become quite anxious and feel unconfident about sharing negative feedback. After all, it can be difficult for others not to take it personally. However, avoid sugar-coating it in any way. Glazing over any negative feedback simply makes the entire process more confusing. Understandably, you may be worried about the receiver's reaction. The best you can do is to deliver the feedback as objectively as possible. Stick to the facts and observations. Focus on the situation and the receiver's actions you observed. Do not concentrate on any of their characteristics. For instance, if your subordinate sent a poorly written email to an important supplier, it is time to give them a little negative feedback. Calling them sloppy or careless does not serve any purpose. Apart from insulting their character, you are not achieving anything. A better approach is to tell them you noticed certain mistakes they made, why they were mistakes, why it matters, and how to correct them.

There is no reason why you should believe your feedback is infallible. Remember, whatever feedback you give to someone is nothing more than an interpretation of all your observations. It is simply your perspective based on the idea of how certain things should be done. Your ideas become the yardstick used for measuring someone else's performance—and it can be wrong. Before you share feedback with anyone, ensure you are aware of the fact your thinking influences it. You have viewed it through your own personal lens. Whenever you are giving any negative feedback, you must remind the receiver it is purely your opinion. After all, we are all entitled to our opinions and have unique perspectives; chances are, there can be missing pieces of information. Whenever you are giving any feedback, ensure it does not become a monologue. No one likes to be constantly talked at, particularly if the conversation highlights negative feedback. If you want the other person to listen to you, ensure you have the time to listen to what the other person wants to say. Learn to be a little curious. There can be certain aspects of the situation you have probably misinterpreted, misunderstood, or misrepresented. By giving the receiver a chance to talk, clarifications can be made, or perhaps they merely need a little extra help to deal with it. Whenever you communicate any negative feedback, ensure it is a one-on-one conversation; avoid the discussion in front of others. Even if you need to provide negative feedback to your partner, ensure you do this only when no one else is around. The easiest way to ensure the other person knows you are listening is by asking them their view about your observations. A simple, "What do you think?" will serve this purpose. It shows you are not upset, angry, or experiencing any other powerful emotions towards the receiver. A little added curiosity at this moment can be a learning opportunity. You are human, and, as mentioned, there is no reason to consider your feedback infallible. There is a finesse to delivering negative feedback. If your comments include all the elements discussed above, it will lead to an honest and productive conversation.

We all make mistakes, and there is always room for improvement. That said, constructively receiving negative feedback is sometimes a struggle to internalize. Do not think of it as a character assassination or personal attack. Accepting negative feedback can improve your self-confidence, self-esteem and strengthen your relationships. Criticism is usually about your behaviour or actions rather than your character, traits, or personality. Do not take it personally because it is nothing more than the critic's observation of you. As mentioned in the previous section, criticism is not failsafe, and you do not have to accept it as your personal truth. However, given in the right spirit, constructive criticism gives you a chance to improve yourself: Think of it as a learning opportunity rather than a means of reducing your confidence and self-esteem.

A straightforward way to check the critic's intent and understand the feedback is by asking descriptive questions. If the comments seem too vague, or you disagree with certain points raised, clarify them immediately. There is no reason why you need to listen to what others are saying indiscriminately. Be assertive while asking your questions, but do not compromise on respect or allow your emotions to run away with you. Whenever you are receiving any feedback, it is important to view it from the critic's perspective. Do not try to see it through your own personal lens. It becomes easier to understand the other person's viewpoint by placing yourself in the critic's shoes. When you consider criticism from a different perspective, it seems more palatable. If defensiveness or anger is your go-to response for any form of criticism, calm down—the feedback is not meant to hurt you. If the critic is respectful and does not personally attack your character, it is not destructive criticism. There is no reason for you to be hostile. If you were given respect, then reciprocate. This is what assertiveness is all about. You can always ask questions and start a conversation about the negative feedback. However, allowing your emotions to get the better of you is unproductive. Take a deep breath, stay calm, and ensure your feelings are in check. To become comfortable with constructive criticism, frequently ask for feedback. Receiving the comments in smaller portions makes it more manageable to process and, therefore, helps us control our emotions and constructively handle the criticism. We all have varying points of view, and understanding another person's observations can be quite an eye-opener.

It is important to ensure the feedback is given from a place of care and consideration. Do take some time to consider if the feedback is constructive or destructive. There is no point in accepting and internalizing destructive feedback. If the negative feedback you have received was solely to cause hurt and bring you down, ignore it. On the other hand, constructive criticism concentrates on the good points and works towards making positive changes.

Your Journey

Think of feedback you have received in the past and determine if it was constructive or destructive. How would you have used the tips from this chapter in your situation?

Chapter 10
Managing Difficult Conversations

Managing difficult conversations is an important part of learning the art of assertive communication. Certain discussions are challenging, but they are crucial for relationships and their survival. Whether dealing with someone else's anger, responding to put-downs, or handling confrontations, there are several difficult conversations you need to learn to manage. Unless you deal with them, chances are the relationship will soon turn unhealthy. In such situations, learning to manage your emotions, expressing what you need confidently, and stating what can be done to fix the problem is essential to maintaining relationships.

It can often seem like the easy option to avoid all confrontations, but, unfortunately, it only increases stress and anxiety. You might be able to ignore the pressure for now, but the issue does not go away. Unresolved issues deteriorate relationships over time. Whether it is an unhappy marriage, a lack of self-confidence, or unnecessary resentment and irritability, these are the consequences of avoiding conflicts.

The starting point for confidently and effectively dealing with a confrontation is a full understanding of the specific issue. This may seem obvious, but one of the biggest mistakes anyone can make is the lack of clarity when it comes to conflict. "I feel hurt about what you said last night," "I don't think anyone appreciates me," "I feel you don't support me," and so on are vague sentences. If you want the confrontation to be productive, it is essential to identify which specific situation led to the feeling you are experiencing. For instance, rather than saying, "I feel hurt about what you said last night," explain the situation in detail. Perhaps your partner was careless and showed a lack of empathy when you described a personal crisis to them. Or maybe you feel unappreciated because no one acknowledges the efforts you make. By clearly stating the situation and all the events that led to the feeling you are experiencing, dealing with a confrontation becomes easier.

Now that you understand the issue at hand, it is important to determine what can be changed to prevent repeating such problems in the future. It means you need to become specific about what you can do differently to avoid a similar situation. For instance, if the difficult conversation is about expressing love and affection in a relationship, think about what you can do differently to avoid such complaints in the future. Perhaps you can hug your partner or kiss them as soon as you come home. A kiss or a warm hug can make all the difference when it comes to expressing affection. This is perfectly doable, and it does not change your personality. While dealing with a confrontation, it is important to understand you should not have to change your character to accommodate the other person. Instead, concentrate on simple changes you can make and live with.

Whenever you need to have a difficult conversation or a confrontation, select the time and place wisely. It would be best if you did not have a personal conflict in a public setting—it will become embarrassing for everyone involved and only add unwanted stress to the situation. Take some time and consider when it would be the right moment to approach the discussion.

A simple way to reduce the defensive tone of a confrontation is by accepting accountability for your role. That said, it does not mean you need to apologize unnecessarily. Remember, assertiveness includes the ability to take responsibility. You do not have to 'win' a confrontation, and you certainly do not become diminished by accepting responsibility for your fault in the matter. Rather than asserting the other person is at fault, it would be better to acknowledge your role in the entire process.

An apology is quite a powerful tool. A well-meaning and heartfelt apology can repair damage in most relationships. But be careful about how you dole out apologies–you do not have to be liberal with them! If you are a serial apologist, it is time to break free of this pattern. Start paying attention to when you apologize and the reasons. Ask yourself if the situation was reversed, would you expect an apology from others? If not, there is no need to say sorry. Similarly, ask yourself if you are responsible for the situation. If you are not, why are you apologizing? Excessive apologies are a sign of low self-confidence and self-respect.

A confrontation should not be synonymous with competition. Even if you or the other person are competitive by nature, do not let this competitive spirit enter the conflict.

The entire process should not be viewed as a race where one will come out as the winner. The idea of having a difficult conversation is not to prove your point, show yourself as the winner, or call attention to the other person being wrong. On the contrary, it is about sorting any differences or difficulties in the relationship. When you turn it into a competition, rather than concentrating on how the situation can be improved, both parties will focus solely on what they can say or do not to lose the argument.

Nothing can worsen a difficult conversation like dredging up the past. If you keep bringing up someone else's mistakes, missteps, or history, it takes the focus away from the issue at hand. It will seem like your only aim is to harm the other person or win the confrontation. Regardless of how right you are in assessing the other person's history, there is no reason you should point it out now. Try to understand that just because something is true, it does not necessarily have to be helpful. Dredging up ancient history is something that you should always avoid.

It is recommended not to use blanket statements during a confrontation. Some examples include: "It's always the same old stuff at every staff meeting," "I was expecting you to say this," or "Why can't you just get dressed on time for once?" These are extreme statements based on past events. Such statements are usually used to express how passionately you feel about the given point or persuade others to see you are right. Unfortunately, such comments typically backfire. They are seen as criticism, and the other person will immediately feel defensive. Rather than blanket statements, it is always better to be specific. Learning to speak honestly and accurately is an important aspect of assertive communication. Blanket statements tend to work against the other person. Avoid saying, "You never listen to me," or "You never help me around the house," and start using only factually correct language that is specific to a given situation. For example, instead of saying, "You never listen to me," it is better to say, "I wish you were listening to me right now." A tense situation can turn into an argument if you say the former, while the latter conveys what you need from the other person.

If you want to navigate through a confrontation or any other difficult conversation gracefully, practice reflective listening. A conversation does not necessarily have to be like a tennis match where each player slams the ball at the other. A verbal exchange backwards and forwards only increases the aggression felt by those involved in the conversation. As an alternative, practice the technique of reflective listening. It essentially means restating what was said by the other person in your own words. By doing this, you show you have not only heard what was said but have understood it. To be heard and acknowledged is so important in relationships. For example, if your partner says, "I feel frustrated that you take so long to get ready and always make us late for our date nights," respond with, "I understand that my tardiness is making you feel frustrated." This is a simple way to end a confrontation from spiralling into a full-blown fight.

We often avoid awkward silences by filling the gaps with meaningless statements to prevent further discomfort. There is no reason why you need to shy away from such silences. Silence is so much better than saying something in the heat of the moment and regretting it later. It is always safer to sit through an awkward silence rather than expressing the first thing that pops into your head.

If you only listen to counter another person's stance, you do not care about what the other person is saying. For example, if you react immediately to something your partner says, it shows you have not even taken the time to process what was said. This is disrespectful, and it can worsen the situation.

The phrase 'pull your punch' in boxing means not throwing a punch at someone even when you can. When dealing with a confrontation, especially with someone who matters to you, it is essential to pull your punches. There is no point in upsetting someone during a disagreement. Doing this escalates the conflict and will make the other person feel extremely hurt and defensive. Remember, a conversation is a two-way street. If the other person says something and you follow it with a counter-attack, there will be no end to it. On the other hand, adjusting your position becomes easier if you take a break and do not retaliate. Whenever you get the urge to say something hurtful or vindictive, take a break.

The Essential Guide to Assertiveness

During a difficult conversation, finding subjects to disagree on is quite easy. By focusing on some common ground, it becomes easier to resolve the issue at hand. Even in an intense confrontation, chances are you will find areas of mutual understanding. By unearthing shared purposes, you can reduce defensiveness and quickly shift the conversation in a positive direction.

Anger is perhaps one of the most difficult emotions to deal with. It is even more complex when the anger is not just your own. This becomes even more complicated if the person is close to you.

It can come across as counter-intuitive but validating the other person's anger is essential. It is important to understand anger is not synonymous with aggression. Anger is an emotion, just like happiness or sadness. On the other hand, aggression is the expression of anger through inappropriate words or behaviour. Anger is not something to be fearful of, but aggression can be upsetting and improper. For the most part, we do not fear anger but do worry about its consequences. There is much to consider, whether it is dealing with sarcasm, insults, other forms of aggressive speech, physically hostile behaviour, or the after-effects of anger - such as guilt, anxiety, or loneliness.

There is nothing wrong with feeling angry but resorting to aggression is undesirable. The first step in responding to someone's hostility is to make this distinction. Rather than criticize the anger, you should validate it. Let the other person know you understand they are angry, and it is alright for them to feel this way. However, you must establish and enforce boundaries on others' aggression.

Is anger a primary or secondary emotion? In all likelihood, anger is a secondary emotion. We are constantly told expressing our anger is bad. It is time to change this thinking because anger is a basic human emotion—avoiding it worsens the problem instead of solving it. Ask yourself, what is the foundation of the other person's anger. The best way to do this is to utilize the listening skills you have developed on your assertiveness journey. Start with the simple assumption that you know nothing about what is bothering the other person. Let go of any preconceived notions or ideas and hold off all forms of judgement. It does not matter what you think. Right now, the only thing you need to do is listen to the other person; they have a legitimate reason for feeling angry. While listening, do not make any gestures that will make you seem impatient or condescending. Maintain neutral expressions and body language.

An effective way to show the other person you are showing empathy is by acknowledging them. By simply nodding your head occasionally, it conveys the message you are listening. Another technique, as discussed earlier, is to use reflective listening to repeat whatever the person has said in your own words. It becomes easier to regulate someone else's anger when they feel heard. It does not matter whether you understand it; the only thing to do right now is diffuse the situation.

While dealing with someone else's anger, it is crucial to understand their annoyance does not define you. You may not even be the reason why they are angry. Do not speculate about the cause based on any self-serving instincts. It is better to gather the facts before suggesting solutions but do not offer any remedies or advice until the other person requests it.

At times, despite your best intentions, you cannot help others. There is no reason why you need to put up with someone else's anger, especially if it hurts you. You are essentially establishing boundaries to the type of speech or behaviour that is acceptable to you. Always create an exit plan for yourself. You can firmly but politely request them to stop; however, if it feels like the anger is becoming too much for you to deal with, quickly disengage by ending the conversation and, if possible, leave the room. Every issue cannot be solved immediately. Accept this simple truth and move on. There is nothing wrong with telling the other person you can continue the discussion later. Perhaps once everyone is calmer, you can revisit the conversation. By giving yourself a break, you can clear your thoughts and regain some sense of clarity.

Similarly, ending a conversation that seems pointless or is not going anywhere is also a good idea. Whenever you disengage, be firm and confident about what you are saying. You do not owe the other person any explanations and, if it becomes overwhelming, walk away. Self-preservation should always be your priority.

How do you handle the aftermath of anger? Perhaps you may experience feelings of guilt, worry, anxiety, or stress. It is important to create boundaries so that these emotions do not overwhelm you. If the anger is not yours, there is no reason why you should feel any of these reactions.

Unlike direct criticism, put-downs can be subtle. Criticism or negative feedback is not usually intended to demean you or make you feel bad about yourself. On the other hand, put-downs are designed for that very purpose. You may not understand the veiled comment or how to respond to it; however, as the name suggests, it is a cutting remark that can lower your confidence and self-esteem.

When dealing with put-downs, the worst thing you can do is try to fight fire with fire. It simply lets the conversation spiral out of control. The simplest way to take the wind out of the other person's sails is by staying calm and just agreeing with the statement. For instance, if someone makes a snide remark about your organizational abilities, saying, "You are such a control freak," it can be hurtful. Rather than indulging in a counter-attack, smile, nod your head, and say, "I can be a bit of a control freak at times, can't I?" Or perhaps something along the lines of, "Oh yes! You totally got me!" will work like a charm. It also sends the message you will not be engaging in further conversation.

Whenever someone attempts to put you down, shift the spotlight back onto them. For instance, if a snarky comment is made about your outfit choice or a dig at your work ethic, stay calm. Do not get upset and maintain a neutral expression. Ask the speaker, "Why does this bother you?" or "What about this concerns you?" This is not a response the attacker is expecting. By catching them unprepared, you are throwing them off their game.

There is no harm in sending a little sarcasm back their way. Rather than indulging in any unnecessary banter or launching a counter-attack, it is better to thank them and move on. Short, clear-cut sentences such as, "Thank you so much for sharing." "Thank you for your wonderful insight!" Or even something like, "What would I do without your observations?" will work perfectly.

Begin to understand the reason someone is sending insults your way. Perhaps the other person does not like you, is envious of you, resents you for some reason, or they do not know how to talk to you or approach you. At times, there can be no possible reason. It does not matter what prompts them to engage in unnecessary insults; all that matters is how you respond to them.

It is time to consider your relationship with this person. If possible, avoid or distance yourself from toxic people. If it is unavoidable, you need a defensive strategy in place. Rather than taking the insult and put-downs personally, it is better to ask what is bothering them. By bluntly asking the other person about their motives, you are effectively catching them unawares. If you have any observations or feel you know the reason, it can be the starting point to addressing the matter.

Apart from all this, it is time for a little self-introspection. Is there anything specific about your personality that makes others think you are an easy target? Perhaps it is time for you to be more assertive. Similarly, do they feel threatened, insecure, or jealous of you? Are their actions motivated by any underlying emotions? With personal reflection, dealing with anyone who puts you down will increase an understanding of yourself. It will also grow your self-worth and self-confidence. There will still be people who will try to put you down and others who attempt to take advantage of you. Whatever it is, do not be a punching bag for anyone. Stand up for yourself and assert your rights. Do not let anyone walk all over you.

I am sure most of us have experienced difficult conversations at one point or another. We need to remember a response is not the same as a reaction. A reaction is usually automatic and occurs without any conscious thought. On the other hand, a response is a carefully thought-out answer or solution in any given situation. Highly stressful situations can be efficiently diffused with solid responses. Notwithstanding if you are dealing with a heated discussion, loud voices, or accusations flying around the room, four elements need to be a part of your response:

First, talk directly to the person involved. When conversing with the other person, use supportive body language and pay attention to their tone and body language. Whenever you are directly talking to the other person, be calm. Do not use a confrontational manner.

The second is to soften the conversation. It is easy to engage in negative and accusatory conversations. The problem is that it does not resolve anything and simply worsens an already heated situation. Avoid any blame while presenting the issues.

Thirdly, be a good listener. Never interrupt the other person who is speaking and listen quietly. Ensure you are not only hearing the words but are showing a little empathy, too. Choose to view the problem from their perspective rather than holding on to any biases or foregone conclusions. Work towards attaining mutual understanding and ensure you are respectful.

Finally, concentrate on finding a remedy. It is easy to focus on everything that has gone wrong, but your response should be solution-oriented or creating a plan of action to avoid such situations occurring again in the future.

Your Journey

Reflect on some difficult conversations you have had in the past. How could some of these tips have helped you at the time? Which of these ideas do you think will aid you the most when confronted with difficult conversations?

Chapter 11
Communicate Assertively

The ability to communicate effectively is an important skill and vital in all areas of life. What does communication mean? It is defined as the process of transferring information for improving understanding. Whether it is verbal or non-verbal communication, it is essential for conveying what you are thinking. If you cannot express your wants or needs, how can others be expected to understand? Imagine all the unnecessary conflicts, confrontations, and arguments that can be circumvented if you are an assertive communicator!

You cannot cater to others' needs if you do not first understand yourself. Assertiveness is not only a tool for self-expression; it helps strengthen the relationship with yourself before concentrating on anyone else. When you are confident enough to handle yourself, understand your emotions, and express your opinions, wants, and feelings freely, it instinctively makes you feel better. It reduces any ambiguity or confusion about what you are expecting.

Your Journey

Think about any personal or professional relationships that would benefit from assertive communication. What are you not getting from these relationships? What do you hope to change? What are some ways you could express yourself?

Say you plan to meet your partner for a lovely evening out at the theatre. The date was arranged a few months ago, and you both agree to meet at a nearby restaurant at 5.30 pm before the performance. You arrive there on time, but your partner is late—again! Whenever you make plans, they always seem to leave you waiting for at least twenty minutes. This appears to be happening every time. Whether it is an unexpected call or last-minute car troubles, there are always various reasons offered. The delay in ordering the meal puts pressure on you to hurry your food, settle the bill, and make it to the theatre on time. It is better to talk about the issue rather than resorting to passive-aggressive behaviour or becoming angry and spoiling the date night. Choose your timing carefully to ensure the conversation is private and meaningful, where you are both fully engaged in the discussion. Unless you address the problem, it cannot be solved.

Ignoring the problem will not get you anywhere. It is an important relationship, and taking care of it is of equal responsibility. The use of 'I' statements can be useful in this situation. This technique is based on research carried out by Andrew Salter during the 1940s. 'I' statements are an effective way to convey what you are feeling rather than hurling blame and insults at one another. It is a simple way to explain what you are experiencing rather than make others feel cornered. Rather than saying, "You are always late," you can say something along the lines of, "I feel unimportant when I have to wait for you, and you are often late. Is there anything I can do to help fix this problem? Whenever you are late, I cannot help but feel a little anxious. I feel as if I am not a priority." Do you see what I just did? Instead of blaming the other person, talking about what you feel and think is a better way to reduce tension and address any problem.

As the name suggests, repeated assertion is to reiterate the message you wish to communicate. This ensures you remain focused and are not veering off-topic. For example, if you and your partner discuss your financial situation, a subject that may not be easy to navigate, this is a useful technique. It allows you to have a calm and healthy conversation without getting caught in manipulative verbal traps, using irrelevant logic, or any unnecessary arguments. This is a simple yet efficient means to deal with the issue at hand without going off tangent. Whenever it feels like both of you are diverting from the issue, calmly state what you think. Saying, "This is not the subject we were discussing," or "We can get to this matter later," can help diffuse the situation. Do not worry about sounding like a broken record because this technique works!

Whenever you need to look at any negative aspects of your personality or behaviour, you may become anxious or defensive. It is natural to feel this way. If you become protective whenever someone criticizes you, the other person will become wary, too. When you become more comfortable accepting your flaws or mistakes, it becomes easier to communicate effectively and reduce any hostility. It reflects poorly on you when you cannot handle criticism. If the comment is constructive and is not hurting you in any way, listening to it is okay. Accepting your faults is an essential aspect of growing. That said, you do not have to apologize unnecessarily. Listen carefully to what the other person is saying and take a moment to consider if it is a valid point. For instance, if your partner tells you that you seldom pay attention to them and keep interrupting, take some time to consider the statement. Rather than becoming defensive, there is nothing wrong with agreeing with your partner if you realize it is true. You can say something along the lines of, "Yes, I agree with you. You are right. I do tend to interrupt while you are speaking, and I don't always listen closely to what you are saying." Accepting your mistakes shows confidence.

The most common response during a conflict or a disagreement is to become argumentative or defensive. By responding oppositely, you can diffuse the situation. You are essentially 'fogging' the critic and stopping them in their tracks. This prevents escalation during a conversation and can make everyone calmer. Fogging is a technique whereby you accept the views of the critic. Start viewing feedback for what it truly is—someone else's opinion. We are all entitled to our own viewpoints. If someone expresses a different belief from your own, it does not make them wrong. In the end, your opinion is the only one that matters. You cannot change how or what others feel. Since it is beyond your control, there is no point overthinking it. If you take a moment to consider it, there may be some truth in what the other person is saying. Although the communication may be careless, do not immediately become defensive, but give it due consideration. If there is any truth to it, accepting the comment will not diminish your self-worth or value. Fogging helps to absorb the criticism and stay calm. When you do this, the critic will back down due to feeling understood. Alternatively, you can ask the critic to explain what they mean. You are essentially shifting the burden of explanation onto the critic, and you can choose whether to accept or dismiss the comment.

If the situation does not adversely affect your self-esteem or self-respect, there is no harm in compromising. If it does not affect your personal feelings, you can always bargain for what you request. For example, your partner may want a relaxing vacation at the beach whilst you prefer an adventure tour at a National Park. In the end, you collectively compromise with a city break to Las Vegas where your partner can spend some time enjoying the recreational facilities at the hotel, whilst you can enjoy day trips exploring the Grand Canyon.

If you are learning to be assertive, you may want to overcome certain negative habits associated with your communication style. For instance, at times, you may not be fully immersed in conversations with people due to your mind's preoccupation. with other matters. Consequently, your behaviour and body language convey disinterest to the other person. To break free of such practices, replace the existing habits with new ones. Every habit, even the bad ones, offer some benefit or reward, making it difficult to let go of them. If you are trying to overcome such tendencies, ensure you have a replacement habit readily available. In our example, rather than coming across as disengaged from the conversation, make a conscious effort to develop the habit of maintaining eye contact, using positive body language, and remaining in the present by giving your complete attention to the conversation. Use it as an exercise to practice your communication skills by balancing careful listening with thoughtful responses and asking questions to show interest and clarify your understanding. The conversation does not need to take long and can be politely ended by saying, "It was really good to have a conversation and fascinating to hear about the projects you are involved with. I look forward to hearing how you are progressing the next time we meet." By using an alternative habit or coping mechanism, you can change bad habits into good ones. Learning a new habit is possible, provided you are willing to put in the required time and effort. A little consistency and patience are traits needed to develop any habit you desire.

Whenever you attempt to make a change, you must practice it several times before getting it right. This is true, especially when you are learning something new. Prepare yourself for instances when you need to keep asserting yourself multiple times before the other person understands the message. It essentially means you need to keep escalating your assertiveness rather than giving up. You will steadily become firmer with each repetition. While doing this, do not forget to be respectful. Let us assume one of your employees is seldom on time to work. You may have given them a few warnings, but it did not work. Now, it is time to become assertive and escalate. You can say, "This is the final warning I am giving you. If you keep arriving late to work, I will need to initiate disciplinary action." Prepare yourself for a situation where despite escalation, you do not obtain the desired results.

At times, a little empathy is all that is needed to make others listen to you. Empathy is the ability to place yourself in someone else's shoes and view the situation from their perspective. Empathy is the building block for solid relationships. By adding a little empathy, it becomes easier to convey your point of view. For instance, your partner is upset that you have not spent much time with them recently. They start reciting a long list of your mistakes and character flaws. Rather than an inevitable conflict, which would only worsen the situation, show some empathy. Let us say you have not spent much time with them because you were preoccupied with an urgent project at work. By acknowledging your partner is upset, you can begin to diffuse the situation. Once they are calmer, you can assertively state everything you have had to handle at work. This is a better way to diffuse the problem rather than it escalating into an unnecessary argument.

Using verbs that are more definite can improve how you communicate. Start using words such as 'want' rather than 'need' and 'will' instead of 'should' or 'could.' This not only conveys what is on your mind but does so with some much-needed firmness. For instance, your brother-in-law wants to borrow $1,000 from you, and he has a spotty repayment record. A simple way to be assertive here is replying, "I have a rule of not lending money to friends or family. I will not break this rule now." Such a statement reduces the chances of any misunderstandings.

Since we are talking about certain words you need to eliminate from your vocabulary, here are some more: just, try, and only. By using these words, it shows you are not assertive. Start practicing sentences without using these words. Say them with confidence and a positive tone, and you will see a difference. For instance, there is a considerable difference between "I'm just a technician" contrasted with "I am a technician" or "I will try to complete this work by tonight" and "I will complete this work by tonight." You may not have realized how the use of certain words can undermine the strength of your message. This is why words are so powerful.

At times, you may not know what to say. In certain situations, not saying anything at all can be the best course of action. There is nothing wrong with asking for some time to think about a request to ensure you do not make any unnecessary commitments that you cannot follow through. Be honest and say you need some time to gather your thoughts. By expressing what you need clearly, you become more assertive. This technique increases your ability to make better decisions.

Sometimes, it can be challenging to express your feelings confidently and concisely, especially when trying to assert yourself. Scripting essentially uses a simple four-pronged method for making you assertive. The things you need to concentrate on are:

- The situation.
- How you feel about it.
- What you need or desire from the other person.
- Its consequences.

Start by explaining how you view the specific situation, problem, or scenario to the other person. The idea is to convey how you view it. Let us assume you need to complete a group project at work. A month before the project was due, the responsibilities of all the members were perfectly assigned. A week before the submission date, you realize no one else in the team has finished their part of the project. Rather than become annoyed and frustrated, the first step of using the scripting technique is to state the facts. You can say something along the lines of, "None of you gave me any indication that you have not yet finished your portion of the assignment. This caught me completely off guard."

The next step is to describe how you feel about the specific situation or scenario. Let us continue with the above example: "It is frustrating for me because it feels as if you do not understand how important this project is."

Now, it is time for you to be specific about what you desire. Do not mince your words, and certainly do not spend any time beating about the bush. Move to the point as quickly as you possibly can. If you feel a little nervous or hesitant, focus on your emotions and hold on to them to give you the confidence to proceed. When you convey what you require, it becomes easier for others to understand what they need to do. It reduces the scope for further confusion or ambiguity. In this part of your response, you would say something similar to: "I need you all to be honest with me and give me an estimate of how long it will take to complete the project." You would then need to talk to the manager to decide the ideal course of action.

The final step is to talk about the outcome or the consequences. Start describing the favourable impact of following through with the task at hand. By stating the benefits of why the other person should comply with your needs, it becomes easier to convince them.

Learning to become more assertive is not an overnight process. Perhaps one of the most noticeable differences assertiveness can make in your life is when it comes to your ability to communicate. Assertive communication is the embodiment of the confidence you feel in yourself and everything you are saying.

The first point is to understand you are responsible for everything you say. Most people are habituated to saying things without fully realizing the effect of their words on others. Have you ever had an argument where you said something in anger or to spite the person you were arguing with? Be conscious not to be judgemental of others with the words you use. Ensure you describe the situation and your feelings rather than labelling people. This is something we learn early on in life. Unfortunately, this is not only harmful, but it can destroy any scope for good communication in a relationship. For instance, labelling someone as stupid is inaccurate and highly judgemental. A more objective response would be to say, "They made a mistake." When you label others, it reflects poorly on you and not the person you have labelled.

Most struggle with not knowing how to make a request owing to worry about rejection or ridicule. Did you ever want to ask someone for a favour but then decided against it because you thought it was a silly request? Perhaps there was concern others would judge you for asking the favour? Possibly you were anxious that if the other person agrees, you will be in their debt. Maybe you are worried your request might be accepted, but they will think less of you. If you pay a little attention to all these thoughts, you will realize they are irrational fears. Truth be told, fears are seldom rational. This is negative self-talk, and it is unnecessary. The possibility of rejection applies to all aspects of your life. There is nothing you can do about it. Unless you ask, you will never know. Remember, someone can always say 'no,' but there is no possibility of a 'yes' if you do not initially make the request!

In this chapter, you were introduced to various tips and suggestions that can improve your general style of communication. Communication is the only way to express yourself to others. Start paying attention to it; this is one aspect of your life you cannot choose to ignore. As with anything else in life, this is not something you can improve overnight. It is a significant change, and the simplest way to achieve it is by taking small steps daily.

Your Journey

Which of the above-listed tips do you think will be the most helpful to you? Which habits can you begin to incorporate into your life starting today?

Chapter 12
Protect Your Boundaries

Every property has boundaries. What do these boundaries signify? It simply separates one area from another. The same logic applies to you, too. Establishing limits is the simplest way of standing up for yourself. It is an imaginary line that helps separate you from everyone else and the world in general. Whether it is physical space, responsibilities, feelings, or needs, boundaries determine your limits. It tells others how they should treat you. A boundary establishes what is and is not acceptable to you.

Personal boundaries are nothing more than limits you have created for identifying safe, reasonable, and acceptable ways in which others can behave towards you. It includes certain guidelines for your response if others do not respect the limits you have created. They encourage self-care, allow you to be your true self, and develop a sense of safety. By establishing boundaries, you can finally distinguish your feelings from those of others. There is no reason why you should constantly be troubled by what others are feeling or worry about what they are thinking. Establishing boundaries makes it easier to do this. These boundaries help develop realistic expectations for everyone involved. It not only teaches you what you should expect in a relationship but tells others what is expected of them.

Boundaries keep negativity and toxicity out of your life. If you have established limits, it is essential to communicate them to others. How will they know what is expected of them otherwise? If your boundaries are disrespected, you do not need that negative presence in your life. Establishing and maintaining boundaries is an act of assertiveness. It shows you are confident enough to stand up for yourself and your sense of worth.

Now that you understand the importance of boundaries, it is time to establish and maintain them. Unless you are sure of where you stand, establishing boundaries will feel difficult. Think of them as your physical, mental, and emotional limits. To set these limits, you must be aware of what is and is not acceptable to you. The first step of establishing boundaries is to take some time for self-reflection by paying attention to your feelings. Were there any situations that made you feel uncomfortable, stressed, fearful, or anything else along these lines? Any discomfort you experience is a sign that your boundaries were violated.

You may not be aware of these limits, but they have always existed. Start listening to your gut instinct when you are establishing your boundaries. Even if you have not paid any conscious attention to this before, your gut knows when things do not feel right. Do you resent anyone? Resentment is usually the consequence of a relationship that leaves you feeling unappreciated and taken for granted. It is typically a sign you have been pushing yourself past your limits or someone else imposing their will on you.

If anything or anyone makes you uncomfortable, pay extra attention to it. Note the feelings you experience, the situation, the people, and the place associated with it. During this period of self-reflection, take stock of all your relationships. There will be some relationships that add meaning and value to your life, while others simply drain your energy. The relationships that leave you feeling tired, anxious, and stressed, are the ones that are pushing you past your limits.

Now that you know what is and is not acceptable to you, it is time to be direct about your boundaries. Unless you convey it effectively, clearly, and without any ambiguity, others will not understand. Communication style, personality, and our approach towards life differ from one individual to another, so you need to share your boundaries with others in a way they will understand. Do not mince your words, make any excuses, apologize, and certainly do not take a step back—you are doing this for yourself.

You do not have to feel guilty for establishing boundaries. You have the right to set and enforce them. No one else can take this right away from you unless you allow them to. Do not let anyone make you feel guilty for prioritizing yourself. These boundaries are meant to keep you safe. Boundaries are a sign of healthy relationships and self-respect. If you cannot stand up for yourself, how can you be assertive? Everyone will have different opinions about their limits. Your boundaries should only make sense to you.

Focusing and honouring your feelings will help you sustain your boundaries. While enforcing these limits, it is important to practice self-awareness. If not, how will you know if someone has violated your boundary? Pay extra attention to your feelings, and do not ignore them. If it becomes difficult to enforce your limits, review them. Perhaps something has changed, or maybe you need to re-establish your priorities. Whatever the reason, tune in to how you feel. Create a plan of action to deal with such situations. Remember, your boundaries must be in sync with your beliefs and values. Unless this element is present, enforcing and maintaining them becomes problematic.

The only person you are responsible for is yourself! Healthy boundaries are all about balance. Self-care is a sign of self-respect and self-love. Unless you love and respect yourself, you cannot expect it from others. Set at least twenty minutes daily for self-care regardless of how hectic your life becomes. Do not let anyone make you feel guilty for prioritizing yourself. By putting yourself first, you are effectively enforcing your boundaries.

If you experience any difficulty setting or implementing your boundaries, do not be afraid to ask for help. We all require a little assistance from time to time. There is no shame in seeking support when needed. Asking for help is a sign of self-respect and confidence. Instead of feeling overwhelmed, it is better to reach out. Whether it is your friends, family members, or support group, your social network can give you the backing required whilst you are establishing boundaries. For example, you can ask them to hold you accountable for implementing and maintaining your limits. This external accountability increases your desire to follow through on your actions.

Your job does not end after establishing boundaries; they need to be maintained, too. When your boundaries are violated, you can feel frustrated, angry, sad, or upset. Unless you explicitly state what you are feeling, the chances of being understood are low. Some may know what you are feeling, but no one can fully determine the reason for it unless you express it. If anyone in your life is violating your boundaries, it is time to enforce them assertively. You can respectfully let the other person know they are overstepping your limits and are making you uncomfortable.

Do not be under any misconceptions that establishing boundaries will solve all your problems. You should prepare for circumstances when your limits are not respected. What will you do if your limits are violated? If you do not have any consequences, it does not make any sense in establishing boundaries in the first place. The action must match the severity of the feelings triggered within you. If you cannot follow through on your promises, developing limits does not make any sense. In the end, you are responsible for implementing and maintaining your boundaries.

Do not be under the impression that setting consequences are similar to guilt-tripping others into following your boundaries. It is not about controlling how others behave. You are merely standing by your perspective and practicing self-care. This is nothing to feel guilty about. Your boundaries are certainly not about controlling or manipulating others and their behaviour. You are simply protecting yourself.

When you start acting assertively, do not worry about how others perceive you. When all is said and done, you are responsible for yourself and no one else. Those who love and mean you well will understand your boundaries. Regardless of how others react to you, there is no reason to compromise on your limits. This simple change will also give you better insight into all the different relationships in your life.

While establishing your boundaries, an important aspect you need to pay attention to is your happiness. The key to your happiness lies in your hands. Assertiveness will make it easier to reduce stress and give you a chance to concentrate on those activities and relationships that add value to your life. After you have established the boundaries, ensure you are doing something that makes you happy. Concentrate on establishing a work-life balance, and do not be afraid to rework your boundaries when required. You will need to constantly review them and ensure they still serve their intended purpose. If a specific boundary hinders you from leading a happy life, it is not healthy, and you can change it.

Your Journey

What are important boundaries to you? What limits do you already have in place? How do you maintain them? What boundaries do you need to set? Is there anyone in your life with whom you will need to discuss your boundaries? What consequences do you plan to set when your boundaries are violated?

Conclusion
Your Journey Starts Here!

Assertiveness is one of the most underestimated life skills. It is a remarkable way to win respect in all relationships. Most of us go through life without experiencing what we want or expressing what we desire. Whether it is a relationship, career, or lifestyle choice, we usually make compromises. Yes, compromise is a part of life, but it is not a good way to live if you are conceding on everything, including the ability to be your true self. Most of us are fine with compromising because we do not know how to follow our desires with the determination required. This lack of judgement stems from believing that we need to be passive and agreeable not to offend anyone. Unfortunately, this behaviour will get you nowhere in life. In the end, you will start living your life for others instead of yourself.

Learning to become assertive teaches you to positively manage conflicts and deal with criticism. It teaches you to speak your mind without hurting others and focus on what you want and need. Assertiveness is the key to unlocking your true potential. It gives you a better insight into yourself, your desires, and what you want to attain in life. It teaches you to reconnect with yourself to form more robust relationships and become a more efficient communicator.

So, what are you waiting for? You now have all the information you need, and it is time to put it into action. Do not be overwhelmed but take small daily steps towards your goal. Even if you improve yourself by 1 per cent each day, it compounds to a significant 365 per cent improvement within a year! With focus, patience, and consistent effort, you can do it, and there is no time like the present to get started!

References

4 steps to handling difficult conversations. (n.d.).
Centerstone.
https://centerstone.org/our-resources/health-wellness/hard-talks/

6 steps to discover your core values. (2020, December 18).
Indeed Career Guide.
https://www.indeed.com/career-advice/career-development/discover-core-values

6 strategies to overcome fear and anxiety. (2018, June 21).
Real Life Counseling.
https://reallifecounseling.us/overcome-fear-and-anxiety/

8 expert tips for assertive communication. (2012, October 10).
Bookboon.
https://bookboon.com/blog/2012/10/tips-for-assertive-communication/

Alberti, R. E., & Emmons, M. L. (2018). Assertiveness training
activity worksheets & handouts.
Psychology Tools.
https://www.psychologytools.com/professional/problems/assertiveness/

Ames, D. (2009). Pushing up to a point: Assertiveness and effectiveness in leadership and interpersonal dynamics. Research in Organizational Behavior, 29, 111–133. https://doi.org/10.1016/j.riob.2009.06.010

Accepting positive feedback is not so easy. (2018, October 18). CloudTalk. https://www.cloudtalk.io/blog/accepting-positive-feedback-is-not-so-easy

Assertiveness skills—assertive communication—6 tips for effective use (2019). Impactfactory.com. https://www.impactfactory.com/library/assertive-communication-6-tips-effective-use

Council, F. C. (2017, October 25). Council post: 15 ways you can find the confidence to speak up. Forbes. https://www.forbes.com/sites/forbescoachescouncil/2017/10/25/15-ways-you-can-find-the-confidence-to-speak-up/?sh=7534257717a7

Daskal, L. (2016, May 6). 7 simple ways to deal with a disagreement effectively. Inc. https://www.inc.com/lolly-daskal/7-simple-ways-to-deal-with-a-disagreement-effectively.html

Eslami, A. A., Rabiei, L., Afzali, S. M., Hamidizadeh, S., & Masoudi, R. (2016).
The effectiveness of assertiveness training on the levels of stress, anxiety, and depression of high school students. Iranian Red Crescent Medical Journal, 18(1).

Glashow, C. (n.d.). 11 reasons why you are a people-pleaser. Anchor Therapy, LLC.
https://www.anchortherapy.org/blog/11-reasons-people-pleaser-hoboken-jerseycity-hudson-county-nj-therapist-counselor

Hartley, M. (n.d.). How to handle put-downs assertively. Maryhartley.com.
https://maryhartley.com/how-to-handle-put-downs-assertively/

Heimberg, R. & Becker, R. (1981). Cognitive and behavioral models of assertive behavior: Review, analysis and integration. Clinical Psychology Review, 1(3), 353–373.
https://doi.org/10.1016/0272-7358(81)90011-8

How to be assertive asking for what you want firmly and fairly (2009).
Mindtools.com.
https://www.mindtools.com/pages/article/Assertiveness.htm

How to identify core beliefs | false beliefs food and body | pathway to happiness. (2018, December 26).
Pathway to Happiness.
https://pathwaytohappiness.com/blog/identify-core-beliefs/

Improving assertiveness self-help resources—information sheets. (2019, October 21).
www.cci.health.wa.gov.au.
https://www.cci.health.wa.gov.au/Resources/Looking-After-Yourself/Assertiveness

Jakubowski-Spector, P. (1973). Facilitating the growth of women through assertive training.
The Counseling Psychologist, 4(1), 75–86.
https://doi.org/10.1177/001100007300400107

Lew, C. (2018, October 15). How to deliver negative feedback well: The 4 things that good managers do (that bad managers don't).
Know Your Team | Blog.
https://knowyourteam.com/blog/2018/10/15/how-to-deliver-negative-feedback-well-the-4-things-that-good-managers-do-that-bad-managers/

Manesh, R. S., Fallahzadeh, S. Panah, M. S. E., Koochehbiuki, N., Arabi, A. & Sahami, M. A. (2015). The effectiveness of assertiveness training on social anxiety of health volunteers of Yazd.
Psychology, 06(06), 782–787.
https://doi.org/10.4236/psych.2015.66077

Paeezy, M., Shahraray, M. & Abdi, B. (2010). Investigating the impact of assertiveness training on assertiveness, subjective well-being and academic achievement of Iranian female secondary students.
Procedia - Social and Behavioral Sciences, 5, 1447–1450.
https://doi.org/10.1016/j.sbspro.2010.07.305

Peneva, I. & Mavrodiev, S. (2013). A historical approach to assertiveness.
Psychological Thought, 6(1), 3–26.
https://doi.org/10.5964/psyct.v6i1.14

Salter, A. (2002). Conditioned reflex therapy: The direct approach to the reconstruction of personality.
Wellness Institute.

Shanmugam, V. & Kathyayini, B. (2017). Assertiveness and self-esteem in Indian adolescents.
Galore International Journal of Health Sciences and Research (www.gijhsr.com),
2(4), 2456–9321.
https://www.gijhsr.com/GIJHSR_Vol.2_Issue.4_Dec2017/2.pdf

Shukla, A. (2009, December 3). Be assertive, not aggressive. Paggu.com.
https://www.paggu.com/getting-into-roots/be-assertive-not-aggressive/

Strauss Cohen, I. (2018, July 13). How to let go of the need for approval.
Psychology Today.
https://www.psychologytoday.com/us/blog/your-emotional-meter/201807/how-let-go-the-need-approval

Tartakovsky, M. (2015, September 7). 5 more obstacles that prevent you from being assertive.
Psych Central.
https://psychcentral.com/blog/5-more-obstacles-that-prevent-you-from-being-assertive#1

Tartakovsky, M. (2016, May 17). 21 tips to stop being a people-pleaser.
Psych Central.
https://psychcentral.com/lib/21-tips-to-stop-being-a-people-pleaser#3

The 7 characteristics of assertive people. (2017, October 26).
Exploring Your Mind.
https://exploringyourmind.com/the-7-characteristics-of-assertive-people/

The importance of being assertive. (n.d.).
Teodesk.
https://www.teodesk.com/blog/the-importance-of-being-assertive/

Wignall, N. (2020, January 26). How to handle other people's anger like a pro.
Medium.
https://medium.com/mind-cafe/how-to-handle-other-peoples-anger-like-a-pro-a1bff7ee9f01

Wignall, N. (2020, June 22). 15 ways to handle confrontations with confidence.
Nick Wignall.
https://nickwignall.com/confrontations/

About the Author

James Turnbull is a devotee of self-help, personal development, and entrepreneurship. An interest in these subjects soon became a life's passion, and his research stirred in him the ambition to live the life he desired and take actionable steps towards financial freedom and success. James left the corporate world behind, and today he is a business owner, author, and blog writer of motivational self-help literature. James lives in the United Kingdom and enjoys reading, travelling, the theatre, and brushing up on his culinary skills!

Did you enjoy the book?

Thank you for reading The Essential Guide to Assertiveness. It is my sincere wish that the book has inspired you to achieve your goals.

May I ask a favour? As a new author, it would be a huge help if you would consider leaving an honest review of this book on Amazon and other similar platforms. It provides social proof to readers in supporting their purchasing decisions, and your feedback will help me develop my writing to deliver the best possible reading experience. I read every review, and your opinions are very important to me.

It may be of interest to know you can keep up to date with news of my book releases, special offers, and details of other self-help books and resources by signing up to Librito's community of readers at:

https://www.subscribepage.com/librito

Printed in Great Britain
by Amazon